The Book of
Summer

The Book of
Summer

How To Stretch Out Those Halcyon Days

JOSIE CURRAN

1 3 5 7 9 10 8 6 4 2

Published in 2011 by Virgin Books, an imprint of Ebury Publishing
A Random House Group Company

The Random House Group Limited Reg. No. 954009
Addresses for companies within the Random House Group can be found at
www.randomhouse.co.uk

A CIP catalogue record for this book is available from the British Library

The Random House Group Limited supports the Forest Stewardship Council® (FSC®),
the leading international forest certification organisation. All our titles that are
printed on Greenpeace-approved FSC® certified paper carry the FSC® logo.
Our paper procurement policy can be found at:
www.randomhouse.co.uk/environment

Design by Smith & Gilmour
Typeset by SX Composing DTP, Rayleigh, Essex SS6 9XF

Printed and bound in the UK by CPI Mackays, Chatham, ME5 8TD

ISBN 9780753539927

To buy books by your favourite authors and register for offers visit
www.randomhouse.co.uk

CONTENTS

Dedicated to my mum, Chris Curran.
Thank you for making our
childhood summers magical

ACKNOWLEDGEMENTS

An enormous thank you goes to all of the people who contributed to the expertise and knowledge featured in this book. Particular gratitude goes to Ronald Somerville for sharing his impressive knowledge in growing vegetables and to Richard Taylor Jones for his expertise in wild animal tracking. Special thanks to the fantastic team at Virgin Books for their work in making this book happen. The team included Caroline Craig for her debonair publicity work, Ben Plumridge for his brilliant copy editing and Gabriella Nemeth for her hawk-like proof reading eyes. Immense gratitude also goes to the team who made *The Book of Summer* a beautiful thing to look at. Thanks to Gwen Burns for her illustrations, Thornback & Peel and Toby Clarke for their cover design, Smith & Gilmour for their brilliant design work inside the book, and Beccy Jones for her work on production.

Finally, none of this would have happened without my Editor Hannah Knowles coming up with the whole marvellous idea for the book in the first place, or without the support of my agent Laetitia Rutherford at Mulcahy Conway Associates.

Introduction

One swallow doesn't make a summer, but a gang of office escapees spilling out of pubs and onto the streets, iced Pimms chinking in hands, generally does. After winter and spring's cool weather, smiles finally break the grim look on commuters' faces as they skip off buses and trains, delighting in the lightness of cotton skirts or shirts, bare knees and arms braving their first outing of the season. Sunburnt shoulders and peeling noses boast of early escapes to foreign climes, and tanned feet framed in multicoloured flip-flops become the de rigueur look for weekends. After months spent closeted away, children emerge from hibernation filling the air with the sound of their voices as they play outside in the lengthening evening light. Summer is here and the heady scent of the jasmine and freshly cut grass whisper a pledge of the halcyon days to come.

The Book of Summer is designed to remind you how to get the most out of Britain's finest months. The pages are redolent with barbecue picnic ideas and the earthy smell of a woodland hideaway that you've built to warm you on the more chilly summer nights. It might rouse you to go crabbing, spend a day river paddleboarding, turn your garden shed into a summer lodge or have a water-bomb war. It's also stacked with crafty stuff too: making a denim deckchair or a home-made bikini. It might tempt you with the delicious delight of a naked midnight swim or equally inspire you to lie on the grass in order to master the art of doing nothing at all. *The Book of Summer* is a treasure chest that glows with the promise of the sweetest season and I hope it inspires you to get the most out of summer's long and hopefully sun-soaked months.

SUMMER'S HERE

Some bank beside a river clear, throw thy
Silk draperies off, and rush into the stream:
Our valleys love the Summer in his pride.
William Blake, 'To Summer'

Early summer must-do dates

MAY

Chelsea Flower Show – the most prestigious of flower shows

Cheese-rolling at Cooper's Hill – the only hill worth rolling a cheese down

*

JUNE

Ascot – the landmark summer event of the British racing calendar

*

Wimbledon – the ever-so-English tennis championships

*

Glastonbury – the world heavyweight music festival of epic proportions

*

Tetbury Woolsack Races – charge up a hill with a woolsack on your back

*

World Worm Charming Championships – a contest to charm a Cheshire worm to wiggle

*

JULY

Henley Royal Regatta – the quintessentially English summer rowing pageant

*

Goodwood Festival of Speed – a three-day celebration of the classic motor car

*

Latitude Festival – where the great outdoors becomes a stage

*

Bognor Birdman Competition – where man attempts to fly with fancy dress as his wings

*

The Chap Olympiad – a London gathering of gentlemen for some refined competition

The Call Of The Wild

I love to roam the wild wild spaces, by rippling river, or lone oasis; Through desert sands or snows on the places, among the far and free. My fancy wings with the winging swallow, my footsteps wander by peak and hollow; Some impulse strong that I must follow, and ever is calling me.

William James Wye, 'Wanderlust'

For me, a summer in our great outdoors is about days spent lying in fields with a view framed by the waft and sway of long grasses and the distant hum of a tractor. When I was a child we spent our summers running wild in the Devonshire countryside around my aunt's home. We'd creep out of our bedrooms at the first glimmer of light and only return to fuel up before heading out once more. We would stumble home at the end of the day accompanied by the tang of fresh cow dung, stopping only to rub our bumpy nettle-stung shins with dock leaves. The grown-ups would cast concerned looks at our grass-stained knees and arms laced with bramble scratches as we silently ate our supper, too exhausted to speak.

These days I live on a houseboat on an island in the Thames and as soon as the flow of the river has slowed enough for me to venture further than the local pub, then I pack up my small, dilapidated, chugging boat and head off to some quiet fields that lie a day's ride away. It's a rare and precious time without the distraction of work and phones.

This chapter is about getting out and enjoying the delights of summer in the great outdoors. It's full of tips to turn a Sunday stroll into a wilderness adventure and is packed with ideas to get you out and exploring the world beyond your window.

> *To sit in the shade on a fine day, and look upon*
> *verdure, is the most perfect refreshment.*
> Jane Austen, *Mansfield Park*

BUILD A QUICK
—— BIVOUAC ——
IN THE WOODS

This is a real Boy Scout activity and it's a brilliant way to create a woody den to sleep in if you're planning to have a wilderness night in the woods. A bivouac is a teepee-shaped structure built out of fallen logs and branches. Instead of being covered with material, shelter is created using large leaves and foliage. Here's how to build one:

Choose where to camp, ideally on lower ground to avoid high winds and weather, but away from rivers or other damp areas. Try to camp at the edge of a wood rather than in the middle so you can see what's going on around you.

* * *

The quickest way to build a bivouac is to use an uprooted tree or similar as the back wall of the structure.

* * *

Start off by collecting as many long fallen branches as you can, breaking off the smaller twigs as you go. Stick them firmly in the ground and lean them against the backbone of your shelter. Use the stronger, thicker branches first to give a firm structure, and follow with smaller branches leaning against them

* * *

Next, cover your structure with lots of leaves and other foliage. If you're planning on spending a night in it, you'll need at least 30cm deep coverage to retain enough warmth.

✳ ✳ ✳

Hey presto, your bivouac is ready to use!

UBER-BIVOUAC

If you've got a bit more time and fancy creating something a little larger and more impressive, then the following will take your bivouac to a whole new level:

> To get started, find two longish branches, both with a fork at one end. You need them to stand a metre or more up from the ground. Place them a good 2 or 3 metres apart, and wedge them firmly into the ground. You might want to use another small log to bang them firmly into place. Your bivouac structure is reliant on the two standing branches being secure.

✳ ✳ ✳

> Next, you need a third branch that's long enough to stretch across your two uprights, resting in the forks to create an arch.

✳ ✳ ✳

> Now find lots of branches to lean carefully against both sides of your parallel bar to create a tent shape. Build both sides of the structure up together, rather than one and then the other, to prevent the weight of the branches pushing the unbuilt side over. If it's breezy, one end of the shelter can be blocked up using the same technique.

✳ ✳ ✳

> Finish it off with layers and layers of leaves, bracken fronds and foliage to provide shelter from the rain and

to keep the warmth in. If you've got a bit more time you can weave young, flexible saplings through the branches to provide extra protection and then cross-thatch your leaves and bracken through these. And there you have it, a bivouac that Ray Mears would be proud of.

BUILD
A
BRILLIANT FIRE

The art of lighting a good fire is a skill that every aspiring bivouacer should master. There is much debate as to the best technique, but we've always had the most success with my brother-in-law Luke's time-honoured approach. Here are his top tips:

1

First of all, be careful where you start your fire. Don't build it beneath low-hanging trees (or in low caves – you could cause a cave-in) or near large swathes of dried grass that could cause it to spread like, well, wildfire. If you're having a fire on moorland, make sure that it's off the ground. Because moors are generally made up of peat, on a dry day it's a bit like setting light to a mammoth pile of fuel.

2

If your fire is being built for heat then think about building it somewhere where the warmth will be reflected back on to you. A rock face is ideal or you can build a reflector by placing logs or stones on top of each other to create a wall. A reflector maximises the heat that is bounced back on to you and also creates a draft to pull the smoke away.

✻ 3 ✻

Before you start building, think about a way to contain your fire and stop the ash getting blown about in the breeze. A layer of stones to mark out the fireplace is the easiest way to do this.

✻ 4 ✻

Always start with good tinder beneath a wigwam of kindling. Dried leaves (which tend to smoke rather than burn) or twigs make good tinder, or if you're on a beach then dried seaweed is also really good (though a bit smelly). Pile your kindling around your tinder in a wigwam shape, adding larger sticks as it begins to catch.

✻ 5 ✻

It's always a good idea to carry a bit of old newspaper around with you in case of fire-lighting needs. Sometimes the right type of kindling or twigs can be hard to find and due to the British weather, they're often damp and unusable. Twisted newspaper simulates dry kindling and gives you enough heat to dry the wood you're using.

6

If you're struggling with strong winds, then building a trench fire is a great solution. Dig a trench about a metre long and half a metre wide. Put a layer of stones at the bottom to provide insulation and help conduct the heat even when the fire has died down.

7

Finally, always clean up after yourself and take your rubbish away with you!

PLAY SCHNITZELJAGD

Schnitzeljagd is a German game that's great for adding a touch of adventure to your Sunday stroll, and ideal if reluctant young walkers need some persuasion to leave the house. It's essentially an elaborate game of tag where two teams – the hunters and the hunted – race through the woods and fields in pursuit of each other.

Split yourselves into two teams, with the hunters being slightly greater in number. Before starting, the members of the hunted team need to arm themselves with sticks, chalk, pebbles and even ribbons to mark out their trail. The object of the game is for the hunted to reach a designated place before they're caught, but they are obliged to leave clues along their way to lead and mislead the hunters, who set off fifteen minutes later. The clues must always lead the right way. If you set a false route, then it must clearly end in a marked 'X'. The signals could be, for example:

A directional arrow made from sticks.

✳ ✳ ✳

A star of arrows using sticks to show different possible directions (true and false).

✳ ✳ ✳

A chalked arrow on a tree.

✳ ✳ ✳

A ribbon tied to a branch to show you're on the right route (though make sure the hunters collect it as they pass).

If the hunted team reaches the designated point before being found then they're the winners. But if the hunters find them before that, then the hunters are victorious.

GO ORIENTEERING

Orienteering is a fantastic way to explore our great outdoors and keep fit at the same time. It's got a bit of a fusty reputation that's stuck alongside 1950s ideas of Boy Scouting, but thanks in part to the British Orienteering organisation and it's place in Duke of Edinburgh schemes, it's re-emerging as an exciting sporting event. Orienteering is an adventure sport involving navigating your way to different points on a map in the fastest time. It's an activity that can take place wherever you are, from city parks to remote countryside.

If you fancy giving orienteering a go, the best thing to do is to visit one of the permanent orienteering courses that are dotted across the UK. They are usually designed for beginners but often include difficult options for the more experienced orienteer. For more information about permanent orienteering courses in your area use the search facility at www.britishorienteering.org.uk. If you get the bug, then visit the site again to find out information about events in your area. Or even better, why not set an orienteering route with your friends – you don't need to be in the countryside to do this; it's almost more fun in the city.

CAMOUFLAGE

With some mud and foliage you can camouflage yourself almost to the point of invisibility. Kids love the opportunity to get themselves permissibly dirty and with a bit of encouragement adults are partial to it too. The next time you head out for some wild wilderness time, let your feral side free by adding a touch of Rambo to your walk and get fully camo'd up. Here are a few tips:

> Mud is the simplest way to conceal and mark exposed skin, but you can also make green warpaint out of crushed bracken fronds or grass. Mix your camo colours and smear away.

*　*　*

Pack some strawberry netting (available from garden centres) and create a large cape-sized piece. Find leaves and sticks to weave into your net to create a fantastic camo cape.

* * *

Customise your clothes by using elastic bands and string to secure foliage in place.

* * *

Hessian sacking is another great camo accessory. Wrap around legs to hide brightly coloured trousers or wellies, or fashion a piece into an SAS-style headdress.

GET ON YOUR BIKE

Exploring by bike is a fantastic way to see the countryside. It's green, cheap and keeps you in shape. If you don't have a bike, then they are very easy to hire – a good idea before committing to buying your own set of wheels. There are hundreds of cycle routes up and down the country and Sustrans, a charity that encourages people to get on their bike, has an interactive map showing you great cycle routes all over the UK (www.sustrans.org.uk). Alternatively, you could visit www.cycle-route.com for even more information. If all that proves too much then here are some of the top cycle routes as recommended by Visit Britain.

LOUGH NEAGH, NORTHERN IRELAND
Lough Neagh, the largest lake in Britain, and with the 113-mile round lake Loughshore Trail it's ideal for enthusiasts, novices and families alike. The trail takes you along quiet, country roads that run beside Lough's

shoreline to provide mesmerising views across the water. As the trail is mostly flat, bar a couple of short hilly sections, it's ideal for amateurs or those not used to excessive exercise.

MILLENNIUM COASTAL PATH, LLANELLI, WALES

Running for 12 miles along the Burry Estuary is the fantastic purpose-built traffic-free Millennium Coastal Path. The area was previously an expanse of industrial wasteland, and has been transformed into a tranquil green corridor offering superb views of the Gower Peninsula, one of my favourite places in the UK.

BRISTOL AND BATH RAILWAY PATH, WEST COUNTRY, ENGLAND

A cycle along this route to visit some of Bath's fantastic canal-side pubs was one of my favourite ways to fill a Sunday when I was at university in Bristol. This 17-mile stretch of disused railway track begins in the historic port of Bristol and passes through green fields and countryside and on through Mangotsfield, Warmley and Saltford before arriving in the historic heart of Bath.

RICHMOND TO HAMPTON COURT, LONDON, ENGLAND

Come and explore my neck of the woods with a cycle along this beautiful stretch of Thames. You'd be hard pushed to call it a wilderness, but there are enough stretches of green park and verdant towpaths to keep any city cyclist more than happy. Wind your way from Richmond to the glorious Tudor palace of Hampton Court. There are some great pubs along the way and even a sandy beach or two.

WASTWATER, LAKE DISTRICT, ENGLAND

Some say the 12-mile cycle from Wastwater to Santon Bridge via Gosforth will reward you with the best view in the Lake District. Be the judge yourself by giving this stunning bike ride alongside the deepest lake in England a go. Take in the dramatic scenery set in the shadow of England's highest mountain, Scafell Pike.

MARIN TRAIL, CONWY, WALES

If you're looking for something a little more adventurous then take on the Marin Trail in Conwy, Wales. This mountain bike trail has huge climbs to challenge even the fittest set of lungs, alongside steep descents to test your steel. The trail will take you through stunning scenery and along miles of narrow tracks that weave through trees and boulders, across streams and down tricky gullies with dramatic views across Snowdonia National Park.

CAIRNGORMS, SCOTLAND

Another one for mountain bike enthusiasts, the bike trails through Cairngorms National Park lead you on a tour of Scotland's dramatic and rugged scenery. You'll need a map and a good sense of direction as trails are rarely marked. If you're after a physical challenge and a chance to explore Scotland's dramatic and craggy beauty, then this one's for you.

CRAB AND WINKLE WAY, KENT, ENGLAND

An easy one to get to if you're looking for a day or weekend escape from London. The Crab and Winkle Way links the city of Canterbury with the harbour in Whitstable. This 8-mile route takes you through Blean Woods, one of the largest areas of ancient broadleaved woodland in southern Britain. To add a cultural sprinkle to your trip, pop into Canterbury's incredible cathedral before you start your ride.

———— GO WILD ANIMAL TRACKING ————

Several years ago I went animal tracking with an aunt on Dartmoor.
I was an uncommunicative teenager at the time who had only
exchanged four grunts with my parents in the same number of
years, so how she persuaded me to join her for a jaunt at the crack of
dawn I'm not entirely sure. The trip, however, made an immense
impression on me and is filed with great reverence in my memory.
I can remember the first sighting of a 10-pointed wild red stag as it
emerged from the bracken kicking the swirling morning mist from
around its feet. I was entranced and have remained so at the sight of
wild animals in their natural habitat ever since. This aunt taught me
the rudiments of tracking – skills like how to distinguish the doglike
stench of the fox from the heavy, musky scent of deer, the difference
between badger sets and rabbit warrens, reading droppings and how
to distinguish a herbivore from a carnivore by its prints. It's created a
life-long passion for early morning walks, to sit still and silent in the
damp undergrowth with the hope of spotting a wild animal living as
it's meant to be.

If you're out in the countryside you can experience this for yourself.
As my love of wild animal tracking lacks the finesse of a trained
expert, I asked BBC Wildlife director/cameraman Richard Taylor
Jones to teach me his knowledge of how to track and see animals in
the wild, which I'm delighted to share with you.

✳✳

Before you set out, decide whether you are going to look for something specific, or just see what you come across on your outing. If it's something specific, then check that you have the right time of year and, of course, the right place to be looking. Orchids will only be found in specific locations in the late spring and summer months; grey seals will be much more visible in the autumn when they come ashore to pup; and Bewick's Swans only migrate here for the winter. Every plant and animal has a peak time to watch it and a best place too: find out when and where that is. The Internet is a great place to get started on researching your what, when and where.

✳✳

Take binoculars, they are your most vital piece of equipment. All else can be forgotten, but not your binoculars. You are unlikely to get very close to any wild animals, so they will enhance your enjoyment of what you see tenfold.

* * *

Other items to bring along include field guides to identify your roe deer from your red, your guillemot from your razorbill. Books are the old-fashioned way and these days I prefer using an application I've downloaded on my mobile phone that not only has pictures but also enables you to listen to sounds as well. These applications cover all sorts of creatures including butterflies, mammals, dragonflies and a whole host more. You would need a suitcase if you were going to carry all this information around in books. If it's insects you're keen to spot, then you'll need a net to catch them in (though do be careful not to damage these delicate creatures), and a magnifying glass helps see the detail once in the hand. If you feel like it, take a camera, notebook and pencil to record your sightings. In my mind, watching is more enjoyable and it allows you to relax and marvel at what's in front of you.

* * *

If you're not visiting a nature reserve with open access, then remember that only Scotland has the 'right to roam'. In England, Wales and Northern Ireland you will need to ask permission to go on private land. Most farmers will be more than happy to let you walk on their land, but if you don't ask you might be spoiling things for others in the future. With permission granted, you have a worry-free day ahead of you.

* * *

Depending on what animals you are heading out to see, you will need to adjust your tactics. Undoubtedly the hardest group to spot is mammals. It's worth taking a moment here to consider them alone, so below are some rules you must follow to watch them successfully.

* * *

Your biggest enemy is your scent. Mammals have an incredible sense of smell and will scarper at the smallest whiff of human, so it's crucially important to keep downwind of your quarry at all times. The simplest way to tell the wind's direction is to lick your finger and hold it up to see which way feels the coolest. You'll need to do this regularly as the wind can change direction. It's also not a bad idea to avoid wearing strong-smelling toiletries and deodorants, especially perfume and aftershave, although with a sense of smell many hundreds of times better than ours, mammals will clock you very early on if you are upwind, perfume or no perfume.

* * *

Keep as quiet as possible. Walk slowly, softly and with stealth and consideration. Sound frightens animals away: watch where you place your feet so as not to snap twigs or create other sudden noises. Dense undergrowth can be very crackly. When working through woods and undergrowth, don't brush through the small bushes but lift them aside with your hands.

* * *

Lie low and don't expose yourself against the horizon.
Use bushes, bracken and hedges to prevent your
silhouette being spotted. Take advantage of all cover:
slightly undulating ground is frequently sufficient to
cover an approach if you lie down flat and crawl. If
spotted stay still, don't look directly at the animal, and
appear disinterested yet aware you have been spotted.
Lie low until the animal resumes what it was doing.

* * *

There is much debate about wearing clothing colours
that blend in. Some animals' eyesight isn't that great
and their colour vision is even worse. I've seen otters
wander up to people wearing fluorescent orange.
The key point is to avoid single-colour outfits, as blocks
of colour are rarely seen in the natural world and stand
out. A mottled pattern that breaks up your shape is
likely to be beneficial.

* * *

Make sure anything glass or reflective, such as
binoculars or water bottles, is covered over. The sunlight
reflecting off your camera is like a flashing warning light
to any wildlife that you were hoping to see.

* * *

You could decide to do a bit of prep by baiting a site
with food. This is a trick I regularly use, and it can
greatly increase the chances of seeing certain species.
Badgers famously like peanuts, water voles love apples,
and a dead rabbit staked out in a field will bring in the
buzzards.

* * *

As well as keeping your eyes peeled for the furry or feathered animals themselves, you should also be looking out for evidence: footprints and tracks are the most obvious. Getting out in the snow is just brilliant for this and hunting alongside riverbanks in the wet mud and silt is a good bet too.

* * *

Lastly but certainly not least, take with you enthusiasm, patience and a positive mindset. Whatever you set out to see, you might need to wait a long time to see it, or you might not see it at all. In the latter case, I like to remind myself that while failing with my main target species, not only have I seen a whole host of other animals and plants along the way, ones I hadn't anticipated seeing, but I've also had the fortune to be outside in the fresh air experiencing the elements when so many other people are stuck indoors.

* * *

Those Summer Nights

WILDERNESS
SLEEPOVERS

If you want to take your wilderness adventure a bit further, then a great way to properly immerse yourself in the wild world is to plan a 'survival' night in the woods. A summer's night spent camping beneath the stars, with branches and leaves to protect your sleeping head is a great way to get in touch with your inner Robin Hood:

In case your night beneath the stars is a wash out, bring a large plastic sheet or tarpaulin that can be customised into an emergency shelter or wrapped over your homespun bivouac (see p 7). I'd recommend one sheet for every two people. To set up a simple tarp shelter, stake two corners of the sheet to the ground and prop the other two up on sticks, with the slope facing the direction of the rain.

* * *

Make sure you pack a few essentials: drinking water, a strong, comfortable rucksack, a sleeping bag, matches, candles, a flint (for lighting things in the rain), plastic bags to stop everything getting wet, a compass, a magnifying glass (to start a fire using the sun), a map, a head torch, essential medical kit, a fully charged mobile phone and, if you're planning on catching your own quarry, a fishing line and hook and a snare – though do bring other food in case you don't have any luck.

* * *

Bring a disposable barbecue or if you're going to do it for real then make like a cowboy and create a proper campfire, with an arch to hang your teapot on and spit roast your wild boar.

* * *

── MOTH CATCHING ──

Moths are the much-maligned creatures of the night. Their death-wish attraction to light means that the flap of wings against the lampshade is more often an annoyance than excitement about a wild visitor to our homes. If, however, you take some time out to introduce children to our winged friends, then you'll soon see that many are as beautiful as their butterfly cousins.

The easiest way to see moths close up is to hang a white sheet outside somewhere that is close to a power source. Wait until it's dark and then position and turn on a lamp so that it shines onto the sheet. Leave it for an hour or so then pop out with the children and see if you have any moth visitors who have stopped to rest. Try not to touch the moths as their wings are very easily damaged.

GO GLOW-WORM SPOTTING

Many people believe that glow-worms are mythical creatures. In fact these fascinating insects can be found in over 100 sites across the UK. They prefer open grasslands and hedges to woodlands and are said to prosper in chalky or limestone areas. It's the female who does the magical glowing as a means to attract the male for mating. Once she has mated, her work is done so she turns out her light, lays her eggs and then dies. The best time to go looking for glow-worms is between May and September, with a peak in July. You will be able to spot the glowing females best during dry summer nights. Key things to look for are places where small snails live, sadly not the larger common garden snails. As these beautiful creatures are in decline, it's vital that if you find a glow-worm, while you can catch it in a jar to take a look at this remarkable creature, do make sure you leave it in its natural habitat to finish its task of finding a mate.

MIDNIGHT WALKS

I'll never forget my first midnight walk. I was aged eight and my siblings and I had sneaked out of the house at midnight to walk across the dark Devonshire fields for no purpose at all other than the high adventure of it. I was absolutely petrified and hadn't even given my eyes a chance to properly adjust to the darkness before I'd turned back and pelted home. I like to think that if we were sensible enough and had an adult with us, then our eyes would have been opened to the adventure of the night.

With a bit of planning and a sense of adventure, a midnight walk is a magical experience. Try to choose a night when the moon is riding high in the sky and head along paths that you know well (obvious but still worth pointing out: avoid cliffs, rivers or anything with an element of danger). Have a destination in mind, take a hip flask or thermos of hot chocolate, find your spot, sit and drink the night in.

STAR GAZING

Wherever you are in the world, there will always be stars in the night sky above. And spotting these heavenly bodies – be it a solitary star amid the light pollution or great drifts dotted across the inky darkness – is bound to give a thrill. Stars aren't the only attraction as there are planets, comets, nebulae and galaxies. For some of these objects the light reaching your eyes has been travelling towards us for hundreds, thousands or even millions of years so you're seeing them as they were in the distant past. Anyone can have a go at stargazing and Marek Kukula, the public astronomer at the Royal Observatory Greenwich, provides the following tips:

Invest in a star map or planisphere (a circular chart that rotates to display which stars are visible at certain times). This will help you to identify the different constellations and navigate your way around the wonders of the night sky.

* * *

Although not essential, invest in a pair of binoculars or a small telescope and whole new worlds will be opened up to you. There's plenty of advice on the Internet about the best equipment for budding astronomers and the staff in specialist shops will be happy to help.

* * *

The darker the sky, the better the stargazing, so in summer with its long, light evenings it pays to stay up a little bit later. Artificial lights in towns and cities will also limit what you can see and if you head to the countryside or go somewhere genuinely dark, you will notice the change. It can be the difference between thousands of stars compared to a few dozen speckling the night sky. But even from a crowded city centre there will always be something worth looking at in the sky.

* * *

With binoculars steadied on something solid, look at the crescent or half-full moon and you will see craters and perhaps the line of a mountain range thrown into contrast by long shadows. Asteroids and comets crashing into the moon over billions of years created the craters. At full moon you'll see less dramatic detail, as the light of the sun is falling directly onto the surface and casts no shadows.

* * *

Download Stellarium onto your computer for an interactive guide to the night sky. It's free and there's a Windows, Mac and Linux version. Go to www. stellarium.org. There are also many useful astronomy apps available for your smartphone.

───── TEA LIGHT BOATS ─────

This is an activity that my friends do each time they go on their lakeside holiday in the Peak District. It's a tradition as well as a competition that's been going for years. The challenge is to see who can build a boat that can carry a tea light and stay afloat and alight the longest. The rules are that only natural materials can be used, but other than that it's open season.

The Perfect Picnic

> *A Book of Verses underneath the Bough,*
> *A Jug of Wine, a Loaf of Bread – and Thou*
> *Beside me singing in the Wilderness –*
> *Oh, Wilderness were Paradise enow!*
> Edward Fitzgerald, 'The Rubaiyat of Omar Khayyam'

Picnics are one of life's simple pleasures. For hundreds of years they have been a byword for precious time out. Art and literature are full of golden images of bucolic bliss, with farm workers breaking from work to share hunks of home-baked bread or the landed gentry gorging on a sumptuous and decadent alfresco feast. These days the picnic still retains a sense of occasion – a statement of intent to spend time with those we love, to enjoy nothing more than the pleasure of each other's company and the delights of the picnic spread.

The idea of the picnic emerged in Medieval times when across Britain and Europe the wealthy indulged in elaborate outdoor meals before heading out to hunt. Barrel-shaped lords rolled on furs with buxom wenches as their wine cooled in a stream and their gluttonous gout-inducing meals were laid out before them. Throughout the late 19th century, the picnic peaked in popularity as a pastime enjoyed by all classes. It was a period when romantic sensibilities were increasingly indulged, and eating outdoors was seen as a way one could commune with nature. The working and middle classes also enjoyed 'Picnic Trains' that came about after the 1871 Bank Holiday Act. These were specially scheduled services that enabled city folk to escape to the countryside or coast with the sole purpose of enjoying a feast in the open air. For those in the upper echelons of society, picnics were a far more formal affair with invitations issued and dress codes to be observed.

Although some might say picnics remain the hallowed turf of lovers, they are also a bugle call for gathering friends and family. With a little planning and a dusting of luck, the perfect picnic can become a legendary event. But if you're not careful, picnics can have a nasty habit of tipping toward the squalid – think limp, soggy sandwiches scoffed while balancing your bottom precariously on a plastic bag. As I've suffered one too many hamper-lugging disasters myself, I've put together the following guide to ensure your picnic is a hit.

TEN TOP TIPS
—— FOR CREATING ——
THE PERFECT PICNIC

* 1 *

The choice of picnic destination is of course a deeply personal thing, so make sure it is in line with everyone's tastes and not just yours. Think about shade for children (if you have any with you), ease of access from the car, room to spread yourselves out and, most importantly in my mind, your afternoon view.

* 2 *

There are a few essential items that every picnic needs to ensure success: a penknife, baby wipes or kitchen roll, two bags (one for the rubbish and the other for dirty plates), a picnic blanket and a bottle opener. Get these packed and you're halfway there.

* 3 *

Next, your carrying vessel. As delightful as a rattan picnic hamper looks proudly bound by its sturdy leather straps and shiny brass buckles, they're a flipping fiddle faddle to use. On the two occasions that we've ventured out with ours, we've ended up arguing as one of us collapses with buckled knees at the stress and strain of carrying its ungainly load. The same goes for plastic bags that leave deep lacerations in your hands or bulky chill boxes that whack your ankles as you walk. A light rucksack, a soft carrying basket or a bag with two padded handles is ideal.

* 4 *

And then there are the contents of those bags. It's all well and good to pack a banquet worthy of the tables at Cliveden, but if you're dragging a load uphill that rattles with champagne flutes and your grandmother's best crockery, you may well have your gathered guests in raptures but it's also likely to give you a hernia along the way. Think practically and lighten the load with plastic containers, plastic bottles and greaseproof paper wrapped with string. If the food is hot, double wrap with tinfoil rather than using heavy tins. Freeze cartons or bottles of drink to keep everything cool whilst also providing a super-chilled drink with your lunch. Alternatively, if you're by a river then tie your bottles on a string and drop them into the cooling waters.

* 5 *

Such prudence needn't mean your feast ends up limp, with cold sandwiches served up on the damp grass. With a few simple additions, you can add a touch of decadence and style to your spread. Carry as many cushions and blankets as there are arms to hold them. Cushions are light and easy for kids to carry if any are joining you. Bunting, or flags on string if you prefer, are a brilliantly simple way to add style to your event. For a touch of romance, stab tall candle torches (you know, those tall candles on sticks) into the ground to mark out your area. Or you could drop lit tea lights into jam jars with wire handles wrapped around the rim. These look beautiful hung from branches out of children's reach. Give yourself some privacy and shade with a home-made picnic screen (otherwise known as a windbreak – see p 58 for instructions).

❋ 6 ❋

And then, of course, we come to the food. Although the slaved-over soufflé looked a triumph when you imagined it presented as the centrepiece to your outdoor spread, the reality is that some things are more suitable for picnics than others. Think pies, hard cheeses, rich chicken liver or mackerel pâtés, cold cuts of meat and floury wholemeal baps; cured hams and salamis, boiled eggs wrapped with a creamy saffron and caper sauce; fresh oysters waiting to be doused with shallot vinegar or a pot of freshly cooked prawns to be peeled and dipped in garlic mayonnaise; or bring a bird – a whole roast chicken, guinea fowl or a crispy moist turkey leg. All are perfect picnic partners and their sturdy forms prevent your feast looking like the contents of your compost bin by the time you arrive.

* 7 *

If, like me, you need something warm to make yourself feel like you've actually eaten, then don't restrict yourself to the contents of the fridge. A home-made, egg-glazed sausage roll that's been cooked in the morning and double wrapped in tinfoil, or a warm potato and chorizo salad, its spicy bite mellowed with a rich and creamy dressing, can turn your lunch on the lawn into an outdoor banquet of the gods. I've featured a couple of my favourite warm picnic food recipes later in this chapter.

* 8 *

You can also take things a step further and turn your picnic into a barbecue. Small disposable barbecues, easily picked up from petrol stations or supermarkets along the way, are the perfect size and weight to add a smoky outdoor touch to your meal.

* 9 *

Next, make things fresh there and then. This one's so obvious when put into practice, but I know I regularly forget as I get carried away with my picnic preparation. Dense slabs of last night's caramelised, clove-studded gammon served on thickly buttered, freshly sliced granary bread and stuck together on site with a healthy daubing of English mustard is a hands-down winner over limp tuna mayonnaise sandwiches whose globular coating has congealed with a transparent and slightly hardened edge. A chicken

caesar salad, its chunks of breast meat sliced on the
picnic chopping board and mixed with crunchy cos
lettuce leaves, and coated in a creamy dressing and
carved parmesan shavings, is summer on a fork.

* 10 *

And, finally, the entertainment. If you want your
picnic to extend to a lazy afternoon and on through the
evening then liberate yourselves from the bondage of
conversation and set your limbs and minds free. Make
it a fancy dress picnic or a home-made hat party.
Giving the day a fancy dress edge makes it even more
of an occasion and an event to be remembered. Bring
some picnic game classics: pack the boules, croquet kit
and bat and ball, or make your own picnic hoopla with
sticks in the ground and used yoghurt pots. Persuade
someone (ideally with a musical talent) to bring an
instrument. Pack the day's papers, favourite magazines
you never have the chance to look at or that book that
you've been trying to find the time to read. You could
bring a board game: these are lighter than you'd
imagine and an afternoon playing Scrabble in the sun
is a simple summer delight. Another favourite of mine
is Yahtzee – five dice, a pen and paper are all you need
to find your way to an addictive and competitive
summer entertainment winner.

PICNIC RECIPES

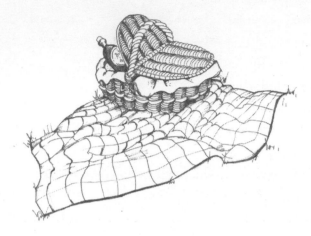

> 'There's cold chicken inside it,' replied the Rat briefly;
> 'coldtonguecoldhamcoldbeefpickledgherkinssaladfrenchrollscress
> sandwichespottedmeatgingerbeerlemonadesodawater – '
> 'O stop, stop,' cried the Mole in ecstacies: 'This is too much!'
> Kenneth Grahame, *The Wind in the Willows*

SUZIE'S ZESTY PICNIC GAZPACHO

This is a genius summer dish served up by my friend and fellow boat-dweller Suzie Cave. It's a recipe her mum Jude has been making for years and an ideal dish for summer picnics. Here's their secret family recipe (shhhh!):

Ingredients

2 x 375g tins of peeled tomatoes

6 to 8 spring onions

½ cucumber

2 green peppers

1 small clove of garlic, crushed

1 thick slice of brown bread

4 tbsp olive oil

750ml cold chicken stock (use water and stock cubes)

1 tsp caster sugar

3 tbsp wine vinegar

Salt and pepper

1 tbsp parsley, chopped

1. Empty the tins of tomatoes into a bowl. Then prepare the vegetables: trim and chop the spring onions, peel and cut up the cucumber (keeping the peel to one side) and finally halve, seed and chop the green peppers.

2. Next, trim the crusts from the bread and soak the slice with one or two tablespoons of cold water for a few minutes.

3. Add the spring onions, cucumber, green pepper and crushed garlic to the tomatoes. Then add the oil and the bread. Mix all the ingredients together and ladle into a blender, blitzing a small amount at a time to create a coarse purée.

4. Put the purée into a bowl and stir in the cold stock, sugar and vinegar, seasoning to taste with salt and pepper. Then chill the mixture for several hours.

5. Finally, stir in the chopped parsley before pouring into a thermos and packing in the picnic bag. Couldn't be easier!

The only thing to watch with this recipe is that it can occasionally end up looking a little revolting (although tasting brilliant). Keep an eye on the colour and if it begins to look a little yellow then add a spot of tomato purée and the cucumber peel – it will add more colour plus a little bit of crunch. Otherwise, add some extra chopped fresh tomatoes and a little more parsley.

PANZANELLA

Panzanella is a classic Italian salad that's a great way to use up any stale bread that you have knocking around. You can make this dish by soaking the bread in an oil mix overnight, but I always prefer to fry it in cubes as I've never been a fan of soggy bread.

Ingredients

400g cherry tomatoes, cut into quarters

½ cucumber, peeled

1 finely chopped red chilli (keep seeds in or out depending on how hot you like things)

4 cloves of garlic, finely sliced

4 anchovies, finely chopped

10 basil leaves, torn into strips

2 tbsp red or white wine vinegar

1 pepper, cut into strips

1 large red onion, thinly sliced

1 tbsp capers

250g stale bread, cut into cubes (I always use a thick white loaf, but it works just as well with other varieties)

Olive oil

Sugar, salt and pepper

1. Mix the tomatoes, pepper, onion, capers and cucumber in a bowl.

2. Gently fry your cubes of bread in olive oil until they are golden brown all over and then add the garlic, chilli and anchovies to the pan, along with some salt and pepper. Cook the garlic through and then stir until

seasoned all over. Put the cubes in the bowl with your vegetables.

3. In a separate bowl whisk 5 tablespoons of olive oil with the red or white wine vinegar and the torn basil leaves, and then season with salt, pepper and sugar to taste. If you're taking this on a picnic, I would suggest dressing your salad just before you eat it, so pack the dressing in a separate pot (an old jam jar is ideal).

CHICKEN LIVER PÂTÉ

Pâté is a fantastic accompaniment to any picnic basket and it's incredibly easy to make. This dish is particularly delicious served up with my fig compote recipe (see page 198).

Ingredients
400g chicken livers, rinsed and trimmed
200g butter
2 tsp mustard powder
A pinch of mace (not essential)
3 cloves of garlic, crushed
A glug of brandy
Salt and pepper

1. Melt half the butter in a pan and sauté the garlic for a few minutes. Add the chicken livers and fry until brown all over. Be careful not to cook them too much or too high, as you'll make them tough.

2. Next, pour a healthy glug of brandy over your cooked livers and set light to the pan to flambé the juices and cook the alcohol off.

3. Pour your liver mix into a blender and add the mustard powder and mace. Season with salt and pepper to taste. Give it a good blast until your mixture becomes a smooth paste (which won't take long at all). Meanwhile melt the rest of your butter in a pan.

4. Finally, scoop out your pâté mixture into a suitably sized ramekin and pour some melted butter on top to seal. Leave to cool and then put it in the fridge until you're ready to pack it for your picnic.

CHEESE STRAWS

Cheese straws are such an easy peasy picnic basket winner. You can, of course, make your own shortcrust pastry but when the shop-bought version is so good why bother? This recipe can be whipped up in 15 minutes, making it ideal for a last-minute picnic jaunt.

Ingredients
500g packet of shortcrust pastry
150g Parmesan or cheddar cheese, grated
Parma ham (optional)

1. Heat your oven to 200°C or gas mark 7. Dust a surface with flour and roll out your packet of pastry until it's 2cm thick.

2. Sprinkle most of your grated cheese onto half the pastry and then fold to create a sandwich. You can add Parma ham at this stage for an extra dose of decadence. Roll out again until the pastry is half the thickness and then sprinkle the rest of the cheese on top.

3. Finally, cut the pastry into long strips, put on an oiled baking tray and bake in the oven for 10 minutes until golden brown. You can twist the strips before putting them in the oven if you fancy being creative with your presentation. Leave to cool and pack in a Tupperware container ready to take on your picnic.

RARE ROAST PICNIC BEEF

Cold meats make a fantastic picnic accompaniment sliced up and served in a sandwich or cut into pieces and tossed in a salad. You can either use meat you have left over from last night's supper or else whip up a piece especially for your picnic. My favourite recipe for cold meat is to coat a piece of quality beef in wholegrain mustard and then roll it in a mixture of flour, pepper and salt to give the outside a deliciously tasty crust. Cook in the oven according to the weight of your meat, leave to cool and then wrap in tinfoil ready to be packed and enjoyed al fresco – delicious.

BARNEY'S SAUSAGE ROLL

I'm an advocate of shortcuts if they don't compromise taste and quality, and this perfect sausage roll can be rustled up in half an hour if you're happy to use ready-made pastry. This is a favourite of mine to take on boat trips up the river. I always choose to make one large sausage roll that can be cut into thick slices at the point of delivery.

Ingredients
500g good quality sausage meat
1 onion, roughly chopped
1 egg
Salt and pepper
3 sheets of ready-made puff pastry

1. First, turn your oven to 180°C or gas mark 4. Then mix the sausage meat and onion in a bowl and season with salt and pepper. This is the point you can be creative and add other flavours: try sage, chopped apple or pear, orange zest, grated carrot or even tomato ketchup.

2. Roll out your pastry into an oblong shape on a floured surface to about 1cm thick and then put your sausage meat mixture at one end leaving a gap of about 1cm at the edge.

3. Beat your egg and then with a brush paint it along all the edges of the pastry. Then roll into a sausage roll, pressing the edges to everything in place. Paint the rest of the egg all over the pastry and then put it in the oven to bake for 20 to 25 minutes. Delicious served cold, but even better if you can eat it while it's still warm.

POTATO AND CHORIZO SALAD

This is another great dish to add a touch of warmth to your picnic spread. There's all sorts that you can add to this salad to jazz it up – it's particularly great with added French beans, which also give it a spot of extra colour.

Ingredients

20 or so new potatoes

300g chorizo, cut into 1cm slices

1 red onion, cut into slices

Juice of half a lemon

3 tbsp mayonnaise

olive oil

1. Boil your new potatoes, drain and put to one side with a lid on to keep them warm.

2. Next, put some olive oil into a pan and sauté your onion until it starts to go soft. Transfer to a salad bowl and then put the sliced chorizo in and fry until lightly browned on each side. Remove from the pan with a slotted spoon and put into the bowl with the potatoes and onions.

3. Add the lemon juice to the oils left in the pan and whisk together before seasoning to taste, and pour this mixture over your onion, potato and chorizo.

4. Finally, mix the mayonnaise into the salad, pop it into a container and pack in your picnic bag.

POACHED SALMON WITH WATERCRESS MAYONNAISE

People think of poached salmon as a complicated dish that requires you to cook the salmon whole in a fish kettle. This isn't the case at all. You can poach small pieces of salmon by simmering in water, stock or even wine for a few minutes, which makes the perfect-sized portable portion that works brilliantly in a picnic spread. I love mine served up with watercress mayonnaise, new potatoes (also easily packed on a picnic) and a salad of fresh watercress on the side.

1. To make the watercress mayonnaise simply put a few big handfuls of watercress, a small handful of parsley, 4 big tablespoons of mayonnaise, 2 tablespoons of soured cream and 1 teaspoon of mustard into a blender and mix together until smooth.

2. Chill in the refrigerator until it's time for your picnic.

SWEET POTATO, FETA AND RED ONION SALAD

I picked this recipe up when I lived in Australia and it became a regular accompaniment to barbecues on the beach. It's especially delicious served with meat that's been marinated and barbecued in my friend Bahar's magic marinade (see page 49).

Ingredients

1.5kg sweet potatoes, cut into large chunks

150g feta, roughly chopped

3 cloves of garlic, crushed

2 tsp ground cumin

Juice of one lemon

3 tbsp olive oil

A handful of flat-leaf parsley, roughly chopped

2 red onions, thinly sliced

1. To get the dressing underway, mix the garlic and cumin together in a pestle and mortar, grind in the lemon juice and about 3 tablespoons of olive oil and then season to taste. Leave to one side until your potato mixture is ready.

2. Put your potatoes and sliced onion in a bowl with dressing and toss together until everything is fully coated. Tip into a baking tray and bake in the oven for 20 to 30 minutes at 200°C or gas mark 7. You want the potatoes to be soft and cooked, and not totally squishy. Remove from the oven and leave to cool.

3. Finally, add the chopped feta and parsley to your dressing and pour it over the potatoes. Pack in a leak-proof Tupperware box and into the picnic bag it goes.

PORK RIBS IN BAHAR'S BEST BARBECUE MARINADE IN THE WORLD – FACT

If, like me, you love to have something warm in your picnic spread, then grab yourself a disposable barbecue from your local garage or supermarket. I was introduced to this stonking barbecue dish by my friend Bahar: she turned up at my houseboat party last year and presented it to a full fanfare of gathered guests. It's apparently inspired by Australian cookery guru Bill Granger and has been adapted to give it an extra kick by the lovely Bahar. This one's a downright winner with ribs, but works just as well with any other meat.

Ingredients
2kg rack of pork back ribs
8 cloves of garlic, crushed
2 tbsp root ginger, freshly grated
8 tbsp soy sauce
8 tbsp hoisin sauce
4 tbsp honey
1 tsp five-spice powder
2 tbsp sunflower oil
1 or 2 fresh chillies, finely chopped (if you want extra kick then don't remove the seeds)

Mix all the ingredients together in a big bowl. Add the ribs and mix well. Let it marinade and infuse in the refrigerator overnight and then whack 'em on the barbecue.

GARLIC AND LEMON BARBECUED TIGER PRAWNS

Prawns are another picnic winner. You can buy them ready cooked and dunk them in your favourite dipping sauce, but if you want to do it properly then chuck them on a disposable barbecue for that al fresco chargrilled taste. If you buy frozen prawns, don't take them out of the freezer until just before you've left the house – they'll help to keep everything else cool and as they defrost quickly, they'll be ready to roll by the time your barbecue's lit.

Ingredients
3 cloves of garlic, crushed
Juice of one lemon
A handful of parsley, chopped
20 tiger prawns
Salt and pepper
Fresh crusty bread

1. Mix the garlic, lemon and parsley together and season to taste. Add the prawns and leave them marinading while you light the barbecue.

2. When the barbecue is ready, toss the prawns on the grill for a few minutes and eat while hot, soaking up the juices with some lovely fresh crusty bread. Simple and utterly delicious.

ETON MESS

Eton mess is the perfect picnic pudding as the mess it ends up in by the time you unpack is in fact the mess you want to serve it in – perfect. If you don't fancy making the meringue yourself you can always buy them in the shops, though you do miss out on the gorgeous soft, sticky, chewy centre that you only get with the home-made variety.

Ingredients
1 large punnet of strawberries
A sprinkling of granulated sugar
200ml whipping cream

For the meringue:
4 egg whites
100g caster sugar
100g icing sugar

1. To make the meringues beat together the egg whites with an electric whisk until they are white and fluffy and form peaks. Slowly add the mixed caster and icing sugar one tablespoon at a time. Keep whisking until the peaks form again. You're aiming for a shiny, glossy texture.

2. Dollop the mixture out onto greaseproof paper and bake in the oven at 100°C or gas mark ¼ for 1 to 1 ½ hours, or until the meringues are just turning brown. Take out and leave to cool.

3. To make the mess simply whip the cream and fold together with the strawberries and a dash of sugar, and then break in your meringue. Pop it in a tub and into your picnic bag. Try to keep it as chilled as possible for a delicious end to your picnic.

Head For The Coast

In the summer
I stretch out on the shore
And think of you
Had I told the sea
What I felt for you,
It would have left its shores,
Its shells,
Its fish,
And followed me.
Nizar Qabbani, 'In the Summer'

Last summer I headed down to spend a weekend at my brother-in-law's new home in Bournemouth, a few skimming stones' throw away from the beach. Along the promenade, two small boys were sitting side by side on the wall eating candyfloss, with the sunlight bouncing off their glistening arms. We sat down a little further along to share their view. 'Why do people always go to the beach when the sun comes out?', the small boy asked his older brother, the sticky candyfloss now gathering in pink crusted waves around his mouth. 'Why don't they go to London or Edinburgh?' His brother remained silent, head in hand, elbow on scabby knee, scouring the horizon for someone his age to play with. It's true there is a

lemming-like tendency that sends humans to the beach as soon as the sun braves the day. It's an easy reaction to explain. The beach is the perfect place to enjoy the heat of a summer's day: soft sands to cradle your resting head and salty sea to cool and refresh.

From beachside dens and foraging forays to games and activities to while away a coastal day, this chapter delivers a bucket and spade load of them. So arm yourself with family, friends and enough provisions and protection to look after you late into the night and head to the beach. If you're not already part of the staycation nation, then perhaps this will inspire you to set forth and rediscover the magic of the British coast.

If you're planning to spend most of the day on the sands, then it's best to get set up with a few creature comforts. In any large group, there is likely to be a split between those who like to spend the day basting themselves in suncream as they turn on the beach rotisserie and those who flinch when a shaft of sunlight touches their alabaster skin. As such, you need to plan for the right amount of sun and shade to keep everyone happy. To help you mark out your territory and to ensure you've got enough shade to give everyone a break from the sun, the following section features a couple of homespun beach shelter ideas.

SHELTER
—— FROM THE SUN ——
WITH A BEACH WIGWAM

Each year, our family makes a pilgrimage to the glistening sands of the Gower peninsular to camp on the surfer's hallowed grounds of Llangennith beach. It's a place of sun- and rain-soaked childhood memories of learning to surf, eating sausage stew under the stars and of tired legs recovering from the epic hike out to Worm's Head. Our time-honoured beach shelter is the home-made beach wigwam. Kids love it as it makes them feel like Native Americans, and it provides a beacon to navigate back from a swim across the bay. Here's how to make one for yourself:

* 1 *

Get prepared with seven long gardening canes and a flat double bedsheet or large piece of material.

* 2 *

Take your sheet and at each side fold it and sew a line all the way down to create a narrow tube that's big enough for a cane to slip comfortably all the way down. If you're using a bedsheet and have kids then why not get them out on the lawn or in a protected area inside where they can paint or decorate the material.

* 3 *

To get the wigwam set up on the beach, take five of the canes and push them into the sand to form a semicircle with a gap that faces out towards the sea.

* 4 *

Next, thread your two remaining canes down the sewn tubes and wrap the sheet around your five standing canes to give the wigwam its outer shape. Push the end of the two canes out of the bottom of the tubes and with the door facing out to sea push these firmly into the ground.

* 5 *

Gather the tops of the seven canes and tie them together with string and then fold and gather your sheet at the top and tie it securely in place.

BUILD
—— A DESERT ISLAND ——
BEACH DEN

If you're after a shelter that's more Ray Mears than Cath Kidston, then have a go at building a proper beach den. This one is great if you're planning to spend a few days on a particular beach and it's a brilliant project to keep the kids, and the kid in you, amused.

* 1 *

First of all select a safe spot that is well away from the high water mark. This is hugely important given the speed that the tide comes in at some beaches.

* 2 *

Next, dig a trench. Sorry I didn't mention this earlier – this is the 'project' aspect! Make your trench as large as your digging arms will let you or at least big enough for a couple of kids to sit inside. Pile all the dug out sand along three sides of your trench leaving the ocean-facing side clear. It's important that you don't dig your trench more than a few feet deeper than the surrounding level of the sand and that your sides aren't too steep. You don't want your hole to collapse on you and any small friends that are giving you a hand.

* 3 *

Dig out a sloping entrance channel that faces the sea and pile all the sand at either side.

* 4 *

Collect together five or six long pieces of driftwood. These are going to be the beams of your shelter and need to be longer than your trench is wide. Place them on top of your trench, making sure there is a big overlap.

* 5 *

Gather dried seaweed, smaller washed-up branches or any other foliage or wood, and use this material to create the roof. Secure it all in place with heavier pieces of driftwood if needed. Kick back and enjoy your cool and sandy shelter.

MAKE
——— A RETRO ———
WINDBREAK

A good old-fashioned windbreak remains the most practical form of shelter on the beach. You can, of course, pick up the classic colourful striped variety from most beachside shops. However, if you want to stand out from the crowd with a design of your own making, then they are easy peasy to rustle up if you can get your hands on a sewing machine. I made one using some brilliant retro Swedish curtain fabric that I found in a charity shop. The bright blues, greens and pinks provide a fantastic burst of colour to our beach spread and are a refreshing change from everyone else's traditional stripes.

WHAT YOU NEED:

✳ ✳ ✳

Eight metres of fabric of your choosing.
I prefer to use finds from a charity shop or eBay rather than buying something new. Curtain fabric is ideal as it's thick enough to provide shelter from the sun and there's usually lots of it around.

✳ ✳ ✳

Five broom handles (available from your local hardware store or online for less than £10 for a pack of five).

✳ ✳ ✳

A sewing machine (though a needle and thread will do).

✳ ✳ ✳

Scissors and chalk (or a pen) for marking the fabric.

First of all, double your fabric over. You could use 4 metres and go single sided, but I think it's much nicer to have the bold print on both sides. Next, lay your five broom handles an equal distance apart on the fabric (best to use a tape measure for this) and then mark a sewing line on each side of each pole using chalk, ensuring there is enough room for your broom handle to slip comfortably into the resulting tube you'll be making. Sew a straight line down each mark and then hem the bottom and top of the fabric ensuring you don't block up the tubes. Slip your broom handles in and hey presto, one retro windbreak to mark out your style stakes on the beach.

GO MACKEREL FISHING

Mackerel are a fantastic beginner's fish as their ubiquitous presence in our summer seas means that if you get the time of day and year right, and have a little local knowledge, you will rarely return home empty-handed. If you've never indulged the pleasure of eating your own catch, then I thoroughly recommend that this is where you start. The best time to catch mackerel is when the sun is heading down at the end of a clear sunny day. A warm summer's evening spent with a line over the pier is one of life's great joys.

Mackerel, with their sparkly silver bellies and iridescent blue and grey stripes, arrive in shoals on the British shores in June and stay to enjoy our non-balmy waters right through to the end of summer. If you fancy giving sea fishing a go then head to the nearest fishing shop to get tackled up and seek some advice on the best local spots. The beauty of mackerel fishing is that the tackle is lightweight and cheap. We've always had the most success with feathers and when the fish are feeding well a dropped line with six hooks can bring up as many glistening, writhing fish. The best place to catch them is in steady or fast-flowing water, so the drop at the end of a pier is ideal. Look out for a gathering of gulls whose diving swoops often raise the flag to the arrival of a decent-sized shoal. Drop your line in and see what you can pull up. It really is as simple as that.

ENJOY FRESHLY SMOKED MACKEREL ON THE BEACH

The taste of fresh mackerel is hard to beat. But if a successful evening's fishing has delivered a catch that even a healthy sea lion would struggle to consume, then a great way to add variety to your feast is to smoke a few of them and enjoy an entirely different flavour.

My brother-in-law Luke, who grew up on South Devonshire's beaches, showed us how to make a beach smoker at the end of a blissfully sunny weekend. We'd spent the night before sat around a beach campfire, gorging on a huge mackerel catch, and fancied doing something different with the fish we had left over. We headed to the sand that morning armed with a small dustbin incinerator that Luke had adapted into a semi-portable smoker. Unfortunately, I'm not entirely sure of the health and hygiene of his method of smoking and as such can't recommend it here, but you can very easily get your hands on a proper portable smoker for about £50. It's worth every penny if you're a beach bum, as you'll use it again and again.

EASY PEASY
SMOKED MACKEREL PÂTÉ

If you've still got some smoked mackerel left and fancy doing something else with them, then smoked mackerel pâté is hard to beat. It's also perfect for the car if you're facing a long drive home. Strip the smoked flesh off into a bone-free pile. Add a couple of healthy spoonfuls of cream, a dash of horseradish and a squeeze of lemon. Mash together with a fork and you have a delicious, soft and creamy smoked mackerel pâté whose rite of passage is to be spread on thick wholemeal bread and munched.

FORAGING
FOR A
BEACH SUPPER

British beaches are loaded with edible delicacies that are ideal for bringing a foraged touch to your feast. With any beach foraging it is important to check with the local Fishery Office to find out what species and quantities you can legally collect in the area. Phone numbers can be found on the Internet. If you're up for giving it a go, then five of the most common foraged beach foods are listed below:

* 1 *

Marsh samphire can be found in estuaries, salt marshes and mud-flats throughout the summer and it makes a delicious crunchy accompaniment to any beach-side supper. I love it raw in salads or steamed and served with the catch of the day.

* 2 *

Mussels are the omnipresent mollusc of the British coast. Collecting them used to be one of my favourite beach pastimes when I was a kid. They can be found in mussel villages on sea-washed rocky outcrops when the tide has gone out, or nestling in rock pools. Clean your hoard by rinsing them thoroughly in the sea and removing the long beard that attached the mussels to the rock. Some people suggest leaving them overnight in a bucket of seawater with a handful of oatmeal to clean them out and give you peace of mind that they have had a last feed. I haven't bothered before and it's not something that my foraging guru Richard Mabey suggests either in his brilliant book *Food for Free*. A great way to cook mussels is to simply pop them in a pan and steam with white wine, shallots and garlic, finishing off with a good dousing of cream. Make sure you discard any unopened shells (an indication that the mussel was dead before you harvested it) and wipe your plate clean with hunks of fresh bread.

* 3 *

Cockles are another of our coast's ubiquitous treats. They spend their days basking on the rocks or burying themselves in the top couple of centimetres of sand when the tide is out. The best time to go collecting is in the autumn months when the spawning season is over. They'll need to clean themselves of sand so leave them to soak overnight in a shallow tray of seawater. Throw away any dead ones that stay shut when poked. Steam until opened and enjoy their juicy deliciousness by sucking them straight from the shell. Also great with pasta in a white wine, lemon and parsley sauce.

* 4 *

Fennel is the natural partner to fish and its soft feathery wands grow wild in our country, despite the plant's Mediterranean origin. Grab a handful from its sandy or even roadside home and cook up with your catch.

* 5 *

Gutweed is the green slimy grass of the sea that dries in swathes on coastal rocks – the cause of many a twisted ankle I'm sure. If, like me, you're a fan of the crispy seaweed Chinese classic, then have a go at making the stuff yourself. Gutweed is easily gathered from rocks and rock pools on British beaches and needs to be washed in the sea and then fully dried in the sun before it can be used. Once dry, fry in small batches, rest on a kitchen towel to soak up excess oil and then toss with toasted sesame seeds and brown sugar. Bingo – it's even better than the stuff you get with your takeaway.

GO SHRIMPING

As kids we spent many a seaside afternoon scraping our nets around the sand looking for shrimps. After four hours of hard labour, we would end the day with a half-bucket of shrimps that, to the delight of the grown-ups, were of more interest to them than us when cooked. Sadly, these days brown shrimps aren't as abundant as they used to be, but with a touch of local knowledge and perseverance you should be able to gather up enough as a taster for your seaside feast.

Shrimps are best foraged during August and September. To catch them all you'll need is a net. Kids can have a go with the colourful ones that you can pick up from the beach shop, but if you want to give yourself half a chance to catch a decent number then pop into the local fishing shop and buy a sturdy triangular shrimp net. As shrimps bury themselves just under the surface, you need to scrape your net through the sand about a centimetre in. Another top tip I've heard is that shrimps love boiled eggs: this is particularly useful if you're going shrimping with kids. Find a rock pool with lovely wavy seaweed, pop your quartered egg into your net and have a dig around under the ledges to see what you can find.

The best shrimping spots are a closely guarded local secret, so to get a good catch you need to do some investigating. Keep your eye out for local shrimpers and copy them. If they're keeping their activities nocturnal then your best bet is to find someone in the local pub or post office and persuade them to divulge.

Once you've managed to gather yourself a meal-size portion, fry your shrimps in butter and garlic, take a cocktail stick and a glass of chilled white wine, and kick back in the sand to enjoy.

MAKING A SAND SEAFOOD STEAMER

Cooking supper in the sand is a technique used around the world. In New England they have pioneered a method to create clambakes in the sand and it's an ancient but still used method in Libya to cook traditional aniseed bread. We've often used it to steam shellfish and slow cook meat.

To create the steamer, dig yourself a two-foot deep hole and line it with large flat stones from the beach. Fill with driftwood and burn it down to white-hot embers. The stones absorb the heat and as the sand provides insulation an oven is created. Cover the hot coals with wet sea kelp to create a salty steam and then place your fish, crabs, lobster, mussels or clams on the top. Cover these with more kelp and a splash of salt water and then seal the steam and heat in with canvas or similar. After an hour or so peel back the cover and reach in to retrieve your supper. If you want some vegetables to go with your feast you can steam them alongside the fish.

MAKE
A SAND COOKER

The same approach can also be used to cook meat. Dig a smaller, one-foot deep hole and put a good 10kg bag of charcoal on top of the collected driftwood. Once the wood is burning well, shovel in your charcoal. This time lose the seaweed lining and instead triple wrap your meat in tinfoil and wind a wire handle round the package. Drop this in the middle of the coal pit when it's burning bright red and then cover with more coal and sand, leaving your handle poking out. It's very hard to advise on cooking times as the size of your meat and the temperature of the coals will determine how long it needs to cook. A healthy-sized bird, for example, can take six hours or even longer if you're cooking on a cold day.

THE GENIUS OF THE BUCKET BARBECUE

If all of that sounds too much of a faff, then get hold of a bucket barbecue. These brilliant little inventions mean that you can transport all of your bits to the beach and carry the used coals and rubbish neatly off at the end of the day. To make one, get your hands on an old tin bucket (I found ours at the local tip), light your coals inside and balance an old grill on top. Alternatively, you can buy a custom-made one relatively cheaply at large supermarkets or hardware stores.

——— PLAY BEACH GAMES ———

SAND SKITTLES

This is the classic English pub game of skittles taken to the beach with the cunning use of ten sand-filled plastic bottles. Get your hands on a heavy ball (a cricket ball is ideal) and place your ten skittles in a triangle. Players have two attempts to knock down as many bottles as they can. The person who scores the most in pre-agreed number of rounds is declared the winner.

FRENCH CRICKET

French cricket is one of those perfect beach games to accompany the setting sun, preferably with a cold beer in hand. As the batter, the objective is simply to prevent your legs (the wicket) being hit by the ball (a tennis ball is best) using the bat to protect them. If you miss, the next ball is bowled from wherever it ends up – but you're not allowed to move your feet and must tackle the delivery as you stand. You can only move if you hit the ball. There's no limit on the number of fielders, and whoever gets the ball turns into the next bowler. The batsman can either be caught out or is dismissed if the ball hits him or her below the knee. The person who gets the wicket is next in line to bat.

Everyone has their own local rules. Is it underarm bowling only? Are fielders allowed to pass the ball between them? One hand one bounce? You'll have to agree on the specifics before starting to avoid disputes.

ROUNDERS

Rounders is another great beach game, particularly if there's a large group of you. Split yourselves into two teams and decide who's fielding first. Mark out the four bases in a square shape and position the bowler in the centre facing the batsman, who stands between first and fourth bases. Get the fielding team to agree on a bowler, a backstop and someone to mark each base; the rest of the team should strategically place themselves around the playing area.

The rules of rounders can get quite complex, so I am going to explain the game in a nutshell. The objective of the game for the batsmen is to get around all four bases in one go or in stages to score a rounder. A batsman can't run past a base if someone on one of the bases ahead of them has the ball or if the ball has been returned to the bowler's hands. You're out if the ball is caught straight off the bat, or if the fielders get the ball to the base you're running to before you make it. Once all the batting team is out, then the teams swap over. The team with the most rounders wins.

SURF STRAP QUOITS

This is a game we invented on a Cornish beach when the strap broke off one of our surfboards. You can use any sort of material that can bend or wind to create a firm ring.

To play, put a stick in the sand and mark out a throwing line at an agreed distance, depending on how hard you want to make the game. In each round, players attempt to throw their home-made quoit over the stick. If they get a 'hook' (get the quoit hooked over the stick), the player scores three points; if it's a 'leaner' (if it leans against the stick), they get two points; if no one gets a hook or a leaner, then the person with the closest lob at the end of each round scores a point. The game plays on in the same way until someone reaches 21 points and they're declared the winner.

BEACH PEBBLE BOULES

If you can't be bothered to lug the boules set to the beach, you can always have a go at an impromptu game of beach pebble boules. To get started, gather three pebbles each (ideally around the same size as an orange) and then find a smaller stone to be used as a jack. Next, draw a line in the sand to mark where to throw from and whoever's playing first throws the jack (your smaller pebble) out into the designated playing area. Players then take it in turns to chuck each of their boules, trying to get them as close to the jack as possible without stepping over the throwing line. You can also try to knock your opponents' boules out of the way.

ROCK POOLING

Rock pools are waiting rooms for animals left behind after the tide has gone out. They provide windows into life beneath the sea and an afternoon spent exploring them can transport you to another world. Creatures such as limpets and anemones attach themselves to the rocks, and young fish or crabs make homes in the seaweed and craggy crevices. Carefully lift stones to make sure you don't crush any tender shells and ensure you return any animals to the same place that you found them.

CRABBING

Although I've spent many a summer holiday watching kids dangling bits of bacon over the end of piers and port walls, it was only last summer that I had my first go at crabbing. It has reached such heights of popularity that there is now a British Open Crabbing Championship held in the village of Walberswick in Suffolk. A record-breaking 1,252 entrants took part in 2009's event.

Don't rely on crabbing to provide your supper. It's more of a way to entertain and encourage the kids to learn about what lurks beneath the waves. To give it a try, it's best to head for a well-known crabbing spot, where porky crustaceans congregate in anticipation of their next feed. Get your hands on a handline with a weight, tie a piece of bacon to the end and drop your line in. When you feel a gentle tug, wind your line up and go eye-to-eye to say hello to your new crab friend.

SAND SCULPTURE

Over the last few years, sand sculpture competitions have become rather popular on British beaches. Each year the World Sand Sculpting Academy holds their annual competition on Weston-super-Mare beach and in 2011 Weymouth is getting in on the act with the first sand sculpture event on their famous sands. One of my favourite pieces of sand craft was one I came across on holiday in Spain: a crocodile with a boy's legs snapped in its jaws. The young sand artist had squirted tomato ketchup around the teeth to create a brilliant and gruesome effect. If you fancy giving it a crack, then head to the beach with a bucket and spade. Mix your sand with water until it has a dough-like consistency and get sculpting.

DRIFTWOOD
AND
JETSAM SCULPTURES

Thanks to the tide's night-time delivery of sea-worn wood and colourful rope-tangled jetsam, the beach provides the ideal place to have a go at creating a giant three-dimensional sculpture. It's a great activity if the clouds have destroyed any prospect of playing in the sea. You'll need to head to the beach as early as possible to be the first to get your hands on the materials. I find that choosing the central part of your sculpture first is best – look for large logs or branches, or even washed-up plastic buckets or pots. Build your idea around the central piece and then collect other objects to bring it to life.

SANDY WEEDY PICTURES

If the rain has washed out the chances of much of a beach day, then have a go at making a beach picture:

✻ ✻ ✻

Soak a piece of card in a shallow dish of water. Meanwhile cut up some strands of seaweed to use in your picture. With the piece of card still in the dish, place the bits of seaweed where you'd like them to be, then lift the piece of card out carefully, with the seaweed hopefully staying in place

✻ ✻ ✻

Blot the paper and leave the seaweed to dry on the card. Next, put some glue along the bottom of the card and sprinkle it with sand, shaking the excess away

✻ ✻ ✻

As a finishing touch, you can draw in sea creatures or other fishy friends.

SHELL ART

Making a shell necklace is a great way to make a treasure of a beautiful found shell or to display a collection of glistening finds. I have a string of oyster shells that hang like bunting in my bathroom. Their iridescent shine bounces the light around the room and they provide a beautiful reminder of one blissful summer beach holiday.

Once you've gathered your shells, clean them up by either boiling them for a few minutes or soaking them overnight in a mixture of water and bleach. Rinse them off, leave them to dry and then rub in some scented oil or even petroleum jelly to bring up the shine.

If you want to get serious, then you can carefully make a hole at the point where you want to hang the shell using a small drill bit. As inhaling lots of shell dust can be toxic, it is important that you do this outside, ideally with a fan blowing the dust away. Alternatively, hunt out shells that have natural holes and use these. Small, delicate shells tied onto a piece of cotton, twine or wool at intervals make a beautiful choker-style necklace and will remind you of the summer's sun.

You can also give your shell finds a permanent place in your home. Large oyster or scallop shells make brilliant soap dishes, a sea-bleached piece of driftwood can be turned into a coat stand or even fixed to a wall to make a sculptural shelf, or else get hold of wax drops from a craft shop and use them to make a shell candle to light up your home.

BEAUTIFUL BEACH NIGHTS

When the sun begins to head over the yardarm at the end of your seaside day, it's time to set up for the evening. Mark out your spot by making small holes in the sand and dropping tea lights in to create a circle of flickering candles. You can even use these in a line to guide guests to your beach-side nightspot. Alternatively, illuminate sandcastles or pile up stones to protect the flames from the wind.

Gather some driftwood and get the beach fire going. After the eating is done, persuade someone to tell a story, read a poem, play a game or even get a guitar out. Share around hot chocolate, stiffened with a Scottish dram for the grown-ups and marsh-mallows for the kids. Lie back to bask in the fire's warm glow as the crashing of the waves serenade the end of an idyllic beach day.

THE GETTING DRESSED RACE

This is a great way to get everyone dressed at the end of a long day on the beach. It essentially turns the normally arduous task of persuading your child to put their T-shirt and shorts back on into a race. Get them stood at the starting line that you've drawn in the sand and lay their clothes out in a line in front of them with a little distance in between each. You might want to throw an extra couple of items of yours in if they're only wearing a dress or shorts and T-shirt. On the word 'go' the race begins. First dressed is the winner.

MIDSUMMER DREAMING

Oh! many a time have I, a five years' Child,
A naked Boy, in one delightful Rill,
A little Mill-race sever'd from his stream,
Made one long bathing of a summer's day
William Wordsworth, 'The Prelude'

Midsummer must-do dates

LATE JULY
Swan Upping, Oxford to London – the annual census of
River Thames swans

❋

AUGUST
Cowes Week – Over 1,000 boats and 8,500 competitors take part in
this mammoth sailing regatta

❋

Bristol International Balloon Fiesta – a four-day hot air
ballooning bonanza

❋

Worthing International Birdman Festival – watch hedonists throw
themselves off the pier in home-made flying machines

❋

World Bog Snorkelling Championships – A wet and muddy
Welsh race for mad men and women

❋

Edinburgh Fringe Festival – when the whole of Edinburgh
turns into a stage for a month

A Summer At Home

My sleeping children are still flying dreams
in their goose-down heads.
The lush of the river singing morning songs
Fish watch their ceilings turn sun-white.
The grey-green pike lances upstream
Kale, like mermaid's hair
points the water's drift.
All is morning hush
and bird beautiful.

If only,
I didn't have flu.
Spike Milligan, 'Summer Dawn'

When you wake up on Saturday morning after a long and heavy week, and the sunshine that creeps from behind the curtain holds the promise of a clear day, then for me there is no deeper or rarer joy than the prospect of an empty diary and a weekend at home. Sadly, such an occurrence is more likely the result of a cancellation than a planned event. As if in fear of a moment of time with ourselves, many of us schedule our evenings and weekends to within an inch of our lives: post-work drinks, tickets to the cinema or theatre, perhaps an evening class, trips to see relatives, days out, parties, mending the fence, and, of course, the over-ambitious five-course dinner party to catch up with family and friends that you never get to see and won't have the chance to talk to either as you'll be too busy cooking. For those with children it's baby routines, nursery and school, dropping off and picking up, and the afternoon and weekend litany of ballet, football, judo, swimming, piano lessons, Cubs, Brownies, eating, reading, cuddles and sleep – it all needs to be scheduled in.

During the heady days of summer, it's all too easy to get carried away with packing weekends and evenings full with a barrage of activities. But there's a deeply grounding pleasure in planning nothing and spontaneously indulging in delights closer to home. There are parks to explore, rivers to lie by, back gardens to sit in and garden sheds waiting to be reinvented as secret summer houses to contemplate the world in.

This chapter is a celebration of summers at home. It will help you rediscover that lost teenage art of doing nothing at all and is designed to give you some spontaneous and deeply satisfying ways to fill your time.

THE DAWN CHORUS

The dawn chorus is a little-appreciated gift of nature that takes place each day. If you've never made the effort to hear the growing crescendo that accompanies the rising sun every morning, try it as it's an experience not to be missed. The end of April and beginning of May sees the dawn chorus reach its peak, and it continues throughout the summer. The songs of our resident bird species are joined by summer visitors such as chiffchaffs and nightingales.

The male bird, to defend his territory and attract a mate, does most of the singing. Typically, birds such as the blackbird, robin and skylark are among the first to strike up, and they begin in earnest as the sun rises, usually between 5 and 5.30 a.m. in early May. Although the chorus carries on until mid-morning, the best time to hear it is the first hour before sunrise – which means getting up very early.

The delight of the dawn chorus is now celebrated by International Dawn Chorus Day in early May: The Wildlife Trust offers a number of events to allow you to experience the chorus in it's full glory in the company of a guide. To find out details of events in your area, go to www.idcd.info. If you can't make it along to an event, set your alarm, open your window and let the dawn chorus flood in.

EARLY MORNING MARKETS

Being a lover of dawn, early morning markets are for me like a meeting of minds. I'm a regular visitor to the bi-monthly local antiques event that opens its gates at the heavenly (or ungodly, depending on your point of view!) hour of 6 a.m. It's a treat in itself to wander around and watch the colourful characters congregating. They stamp vintage-shod feet and throw back brightly dyed and tobacco-stained hair as they cackle in delight at seeing each other again. They are wearing their best tweed jackets or layered country skirts in anticipation of an escape from their fusty antique shops to spend a day in the open air. Fingerless gloves provide warmth while allowing for expert fingers to pry through comrades' offerings. Hands clasp around polystyrene cups, cold breath mingles with the rising steam.

Whether your delight is found in the trawling of the morning catch or in the scent of a thousand bouquets, below is a guide to some of our country's best early morning markets:

New Covent Garden Market, London

* * *

Columbia Road Flower Market, London

* * *

Billingsgate Fish Market, London

* * *

Sunbury Antiques Market, Kempton Park, Surrey

* * *

Bristol Farmers' Market

* * *

Looe Fish Market, Cornwall

* * *

Barrowland Market (or The Barras), Glasgow – sells anything and everything

* * *

Cardiff Central Market – fresh Welsh foods and much more

* * *

Grimsby Fish Market, Grimsby

HAVE A PICFAST

A picfast (a cunning blend of picnic and breakfast) is exactly what it says on the tin. I think enjoying breakfast on a picnic blanket is one of life's overlooked pleasures. It's the time of day when you have the park to yourself, when the duck pond lies undisturbed by the splash and scream of small children. It's when you can enjoy a park view softened by the morning mist and before inconsiderate individuals have littered the green with rubbish.

MAKE AN INSTANT HAMMOCK

A sign that you have become a master of the art of doing nothing is when you can spend a day in a hammock. It's a symbol of desert-island escapism and tropical retreats and the ultimate in garden relaxation. You can, of course, head to the shops or jump on the Internet to buy one, but you can also make one in an instant with this cunning technique:

WHAT YOU NEED:

✳ ✳ ✳

A double duvet cover or similar-sized piece of material – a large curtain is ideal.

✳ ✳ ✳

Two ropes about 5 metres long.

✳ 1 ✳

To get started, you need to choose somewhere safe to hang the hammock. A couple of palm trees would be ideal, though an oak trunk next to a sturdy fence is also a winner.

✳ 2 ✳

Tie a simple knot at either end of your curtain or duvet cover.

✳ 3 ✳

Next, double over one of your ropes and tie a knot to create a loop. Run your loop around the tree or post and pass one end through the other, pulling tight to fix securely in place.

* 4 *

Create another loop using the dangling end of the loop and then thread one of the large material knots through this, pulling it tight.

* 5 *

Finally, attach the other end of the hammock to another tree or post in exactly the same way, before kicking back to enjoy.

——— CLOUD SPOTTING ———

A few of our sky's favourites for you to spot while relaxing in your hammock.

CIRRUS

CUMULUS

STRATUS

MINDLESS ENTERTAINMENT

Sometimes, doing absolutely nothing at all is just a bit too hard for our minds to cope with. For those who lead an action-packed life and are regularly found drumming their fingers or tapping their feet, the thought of doing nothing and not being asleep is almost impossible to comprehend. That's why it's useful to have a couple of games up your sleeve to keep your mind entertained just enough to stop you leaping up and starting some sort of ambitious project. Here are some of my favourites:

✳ ✳ ✳

Play hangman.

✳ ✳ ✳

Do the crossword.

✳ ✳ ✳

Learn a poem that you can recite on call.

✳ ✳ ✳

Master origami.

✳ ✳ ✳

Learn a magic trick to impress the guests at your next dinner party.

✳ ✳ ✳

Meditate.

✳ ✳ ✳

Count sheep and find yourself slowly drifting off to sleep.

Homespun Fun

MAKING
—— AND ——
FLYING A KITE

Making a kite is a childhood rite of passage. There are lots of different methods, but with the following guidelines you should be able to put one together using the contents of your kitchen cupboards:

* * *

First of all, gather together a plastic bag, two thin, light, straight sticks, ribbons or streamers, string, tape and scissors.

* * *

Once set up, cut a traditional kite-shaped piece from the plastic bag – this should be as large as you can make it.

* * *

Position the sticks over the kite shape so that they're lined up with each corner, and then bind them together where they cross, using string.

* * *

Then reposition the sticks and stretch the plastic as much as possible before taping them in place. If you don't have any tape you can tie the plastic in place using string.

* * *

When you've got your basic kite shape ready, tie a piece of string from one side of the cross stick to the other leaving a fair amount of slack. Then tie a much longer piece of string to the bottom of the longest stick and then tie this to the centre of the slackened piece of string to create a triangle-like shape, leaving the rest of the string hanging down.

* * *

You can decorate the bottom of your kite with ribbons or streamers that also function to keep it weighted down and flying the right way up.

* * *

As long as there is a healthy amount of wind in the air, you should now be ready to fly.

SET UP A STREET STALL

Kids love to play shop and a great way to encourage this entrepreneurial spirit is to get them to set up a stall selling their wares. Cookies and fairy cakes are always a winner or get them to sell something they've made or even their old toys. If you live in a safe neighbourhood then they can set up the stall in your front garden or doorway, otherwise get them to invite friends and neighbours in to browse their wares.

BECOME A
CHALK STREET ARTIST

Liberate your creative prowess and arm yourself with a pack of chalks and do some covert chalk artistry. If you're feeling a little unsure of yourself at first, then practise on your patio. If you've got some young'uns around then encourage them to chalk up a giant game of snakes and ladders or a colourfully decorated hopscotch course. This might fill the more house-proud person with fear, but chalk is easily scrubbed off with a broom and a bit of water. You could always turn it into a romantic message for someone. In his love-struck university years a friend of mine chalked the following outside a new girlfriend's house: 'The rain might wash this note away but my love will always stay'.

FROZEN OUTFIT
COMPETITION

This is a great game to cool you down on a hot day. Soak a couple of T-shirts and shorts in water, fold them up and then pop them in the freezer. Once frozen, hand them out and then on the word 'go' everyone has to race to be the first to get them on.

SUMMER
HAT TAG

This is a great twist on the traditional game of tag. In this format, whoever's 'it' has to wear the hat and is the one being chased. The aim of the game is to keep the hat on the longest. Anyone who can snatch the hat puts it on, and, has as a two-second lead before the others lay chase.

WATER-BOMB WAR

To entertain a big group of children on a sunny day, get your hands on some water bombs. These are really cheap and usually available from local toyshops. They're essentially mini balloons filled with water. Divide your bombs equally between two teams and get them to go to their bases. On the word 'go' the kids have to bombard each other with their water balloons. The team that stays the driest is the winner.

FLOUR AND EGG FIGHT

This used to be a forbidden but much-anticipated marker of the end of the summer school term. Each year, as the countdown to the summer holidays began, stern warnings were issued in morning assembly as to the consequences for those who might be tempted to engage in flour and egg wars. Without fail, the departing year group, in pure delight at the liberation from the school's rules, would flout these warnings and decorate the school in a thick coating of cake mix.

Flour and egg fights are brilliant but thoroughly messy ways to indulge the kids. If, like me, you enjoy encouraging the occasional bout of feral behaviour, then arm them with half a dozen eggs and a bag of flour each, take them to the local park or field and watch chaos commence.

HOLD A
—— FANCY DRESS ——
BIKE PARADE

A bike is often a child's proudest possession. The intense sense of
freedom and achievement when those stabilizers are finally taken
off places these machines of liberation firmly on the pedestal.
A great way to fill a sunny afternoon is to encourage your kids and
any others that you can muster to decorate their bikes in anticipation
of an early evening fancy dress bike parade.

Wind the bars with ribbons and streamers, attach cardboard
shapes and faces to the front and back, or you can even dress them
up in your clothes: a jumper fits neatly on the handlebars and if
you have a big skirt, this can be used to cover the top of the frame.
Just be careful it can't get caught in the wheels. Once set, whistles
and flags at the ready, and off they go.

MAKE A
MINI GARDEN
ZIP WIRE

This is a fantastic way to provide a summer's worth of garden entertainment. The idea is to create a zip wire for you to send refreshments down to your garden chair or for your kids to send their toys and snacks from one end of the garden to the other. Here's how to make one:

✳ ✳ ✳

First of all, decide where your zip wire is going to go. You might want to string it from an upstairs window to a tree in the garden, or you could even customize a washing line. You just need to ensure that the slope is gentle enough that the car doesn't whizz down too quickly and upset it's contents, but not so gentle that it doesn't run.

✳ ✳ ✳

Next, you need to build your car. You can use a basket or even get your kids to create one out of a cardboard box.

✳ ✳ ✳

Once finished, let your kids enjoy the delight of whizzing everything from their teddy to their towel down your garden zip wire.

GROW THE PERFECT SUMMER LAWN

The soft, springy sponginess of a beautiful lawn is impossible to beat when it comes to garden lounging. However, if, like mine, your grass is far from ready for the long summer months, then here's a few simple steps to achieving verdant perfection:

1

The main reason that some lawns better resemble a barren dust bowl than a bowling green is sunshine. Unless you are the owners of Arsenal stadium and can wheel in a fake sun, then pruning might be the better option. If you're struggling with a lack of sunlight then review the shadow thrown by garden sheds, hedges, fences and trees, and attempt to address these before spending a fortune on fertilizer and seed.

2

Lawns benefit from being aerated once a year, ideally in the spring. Aerating a lawn means peppering it with 10cm deep holes all over. This can be done with a garden fork, though there is comedy in watching someone else dance around the lawn wearing spiky shoes (which can be picked up at most garden centres).

3

Once it's had a good piercing, it's good to douse it in lawn sand to help with drainage and to prevent things

getting too claggy when the rains come. Cover any
bare patches with lawn seed.

* 4 *

Finally, become a better mower. For a lawn to truly
come into it's own during the summer months, it really
needs to be mown once a week.

TURN YOUR
GARDEN SHED INTO
A SUMMERHOUSE

In my mind, garden sheds are a suburban eyesore and general
dumping ground for the stuff no one wants to see. Which is such a
shame, as with a touch of paint and some creative interior work
they can be transformed into a tranquil retreat. This summer, why
not have a go at bringing the indoors out and turning your garden
shed into an elegant summerhouse.

Once you've done your clear-out and decided where to store the
lawnmower and garden tools, you can then get on with the fun
part. If your shed is looking a little weathered then give it a fresh
feel with some summerhouse paint shades. Sand off any existing
paint and for a longer-lasting result, give the wood a treatment and
then paint with a primer before the final colour. You can achieve a
vintage look with muted creams, duck egg blues and National
Trust greens, or go for something bright and fresh by using cheery
circus colours. If you want to feel more outside than in, then with a
little carpentry you can turn the front of your summerhouse into a

giant door. By doing this you create a three-sided outdoor room that can be shut back up when the weather warrants it.

Once the exterior is finished, let your creativity run free on the inside. Trawl junk and charity shops for old wooden tables and chairs that can be bought back to life with a fresh lick of paint. Soften the feel by covering the floor with rugs and cushions. Find a battered old sofa or armchair whose house days are numbered and add a wonderfully shabby vintage touch to your outdoor room.

BUILD A LIVING WILLOW WIGWAM

Willow is a fantastic material to work with as it's flexible form means that you can weave it into all sorts of shapes. By building a living willow wigwam in your garden you'll create a quiet place out of the sun or a den to keep your kids entertained for years to come. Here's how to give it a go:

* 1 *

Get your hands on 10 to 15 recently cut 2-metre willow whips to create your uprights (they need to be recently cut to ensure they'll grow). You'll also need about 30 willow rods for weaving. Go online to find your local supplier (who may well sell wigwam kits). The best time to plant your willow is during the winter and early spring when the tree is normally dormant.

* 2 *

Find a spot where you're happy for your willow wigwam to permanently live.

* 3 *

Mark out your wigwam circle by pushing the uprights firmly into the ground, making sure you leave a space for the door in the direction you want it to face.

* 4 *

Next (and you might need a chair or stepladder for this unless you are impressively tall), gather the tops of your uprights together and tie them in place using some twine.

* 5 *

Now weave your other willow rods in and out of your uprights to create a solid shape.

* 6 *

Finally, relax and wait for your willow wigwam to start to grow. If you keep it well watered you'll be surprised at how quickly it shoots up. The first year's growth can be up to 2 metres. Once new branches start to form, keep trimming off any that stick out, and use what you trim to weave back in, which will add strength to your structure.

BUILD A TREE CHAIR

Sadly, not all of us are Bob the Builders who can knock up a tree house at the weekend. With this in mind, move on from kicking yourself for failing to be a superdad/mum/aunt/uncle and do something selfish instead – stick a chair in a tree and create your own personal private hideaway. This might sound ridiculous, but a friend of mine bound an old rattan chair to the boughs of a tree and created a magical hidden eyrie with an astounding view across the countryside. It remains his chosen spot to read the Sunday papers and he winds up the rope ladder once he's up there to prevent the kids climbing up and disturbing his sanctuary. Now this flouts all sorts of health and safety rules, so the obligatory note on doing this at your own risk is required. Be sensible in terms of where you choose to put your chair, and remember that it is *definitely* a grown-up place and not somewhere for the kids to play.

TURN YOUR POND INTO A WILD SWIMMING POOL

For those that are lucky enough to have a large pond in their garden, why not bring wild swimming home and rename it as a natural swimming pool. If it's clogged up with pondweed then give it a bit of a clear-out. Position some steps if necessary and enjoy a relaxing natural dip.

GROW SUNFLOWERS

Sunflowers are a great way to introduce yourself to the magic of growing things. Certain varieties, such as the Russian Giant, can grow up to 3 metres tall, and you can watch their daily climb as they spiral up to the sky. Incas used to worship the image of the sunflower as a symbol of the sun god. It's easy to see why: the process of heliotropism means that a sunflower's golden face turns east at sunrise and follows the westward course of the sun throughout the day, bowing its lion-like head in sleep at sunset.

It's always best to sow your sunflower seeds in May and start them off inside or in a greenhouse if you have one. Prepare a small pot with compost, push your seed 3cm in, cover with soil, water and then leave in a sunny position. Germination normally takes between 10 and 14 days, and once three full leaves have developed the plant is ready to live outside. If you become protective of its young leaves, you might want to bring it in for the first couple of nights if it's particularly chilly. Once your sunflower starts to get too big for its pot, transplant it into the ground in full sun, ideally somewhere in front of a fence or wall that can act as a supporting stake. You can grow sunflowers in pots, but you'll need to ensure they have enough support to prevent the pot toppling over. Water well throughout the year as they are thirsty big things.

———— MAKE A TREE SWING ————

There is a sweet, bucolic pleasure in rocking on a swing that hangs from the strong boughs of a tree. It's made even sweeter when you've made the swing yourself. Here are a few simple tips:

✳ ✳ ✳

Choose a tall, strong tree with a suitable horizontal branch.

✳ ✳ ✳

Make your seat from a piece of quality rot-proof hardwood. You want something that's about 60cm long by 30cm wide, with enough thickness to hold a large amount of weight.

✳ ✳ ✳

Drill two holes at either end and thread a piece of strong rope through the first hole and then up through the second hole. Tie this back onto the rope to create a triangle shape – see diagram. Do the same on the other side.

✳ ✳ ✳

Hang your swing by tying the other ends of the rope over your chosen bough, ensuring they are very securely in place.

LIGHT UP YOUR GARDEN

MAKE A RUSTIC LANTERN

This is the simplest garden light you can make, and its simplicity is what gives it that special rustic charm. Get your hands on some old jam jars and remove the labels. Tie fire retardant string around the rims and then attach loops to act as hangers. Fill the jars half full of water and float a tea light in each, before hanging them somewhere safe to light up your garden.

MAKE PAPER BAG LAMPS

Paper bag lamps are another simple but magical touch to add to your garden, particularly if you're planning an al fresco feast. Find some paper bags that stand up on their own and spray them all over with fire retardant spray (you can get hold of this from your local hardware store). Weigh them down with sand or a stone and put a tea light inside to create a warm and magical glow. Position your paper bags to create a pathway to lead to your table.

TIN-CAN LANTERNS

Clean out an old tin can and remove the label from the outside. Create patterns on the can by piercing it all over using a skewer (being very careful not to include your hand in the skewering). Pierce holes either side of the top of the tin and create a loop with some more string to hang the can from. For an extra touch, you can paint the can using colourful metal paint.

If you are feeling lazy, you can always buy an old-fashioned paraffin lantern.

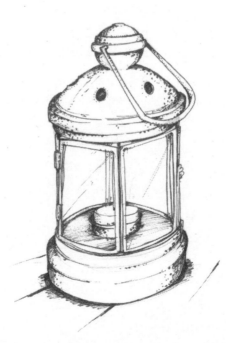

Crafty Days

> *It is full summer now, the heart of June;*
> *Not yet the sunburnt reapers are astir*
> *Upon the upland meadow where too soon*
> *Rich autumn time, the season's usurer,*
> *Will lend his hoarded gold to all the trees,*
> *And see his treasure scattered by the wild and*
> *spendthrift breeze.*
> Oscar Wilde, 'The Garden Of Eros'

The rediscovery of craft is in many ways a reaction to the commercial culture that pervaded the nineties and early noughties. The resulting global crash has put traditional ways of living into even greater focus. The craft movement is also an act of rebellion against celebrity culture: while children's TV presenters and politicians are exposed taking part in any number of iniquitous activities, mastering the art of cross stitch while sipping a cup of Earl Grey with the girls suddenly feels deeply subversive.

Beyond all that, there is a deeper emotional reason why people have been dusting off their sewing boxes and reaching for their hammers – making something yourself is such a satisfying way to fill your time. There's a kind of smug wholesomeness to be felt while whipping up your latest creation, entertaining yourself with thoughts of friends lying comatose in front of the television or at the local pub. It's also something that will get you plaudits.

Brownie points are awarded to those who turn up to dinner parties with a home-made slab of quince cheese or a hand-printed tea towel rather than a bottle of wine grabbed from the supermarket on the way.

The projects that I've selected here are about finding new ways to re-invent old stuff and will give your summer a homespun flavour.

RE-INVENT A GARDEN CHAIR

A rummage around your local car boot sale or charity shop is bound to throw up an old canvas director's chair. You know the ones I mean, something that's looking a bit moth-eaten or ragged, and generally past its best. Instead of consigning it to the scrapheap, grab it and give it a new lease of life. Anything with a canvas seat and back will do – the holy grail would be an old deckchair, but these are very hard to find.

First, you need to decide what fabric you're going to re-upholster with. This is the fun part: an old pair of jeans or cords makes a fantastic, novel and sturdy chair material, as would some faded velvet curtains. Whatever you use must be strong enough to comfortably hold someone's weight. One of my favourite places to buy fabric for the garden is www.deckchairstripes.com. They have a fantastic collection of retro designs to brighten up any garden.

To strip off the old fabric from your chair, you'll probably need to partially dismantle the woodwork. Remove the screws and staples from the fabric and use it as a template for your chosen material. If you're using old trousers, you'll need to cut them up and sew pieces together. The complexity of the job will vary depending on how your chair is put together, but just follow what was done originally. Before you put it all back together, you might want to touch the wood up with a fresh lick of paint to give it a really smart finish.

MAKE A TOWEL BEACH BAG

When summer's here, the last thing you want to be doing is lugging a heavy, clunky bag around. This idea is really simple to do and turns your towel into a bag for a day on the beach or by the river:

* 1 *

You'll need a beach towel and a smaller face towel (you can always dye old ones to give them a new lease of life).

* 2 *

Cut two 10cm strips off the edge of the smaller towel.

* 3 *

Sew the bottom edge of the smaller towel onto the centre of one end of the bigger one, leaving the top of it open.

* 4 *

To make the handles, use the two 10cm strips and roll them into long, thick cords. Sew them onto the outside of the pocket that you have created so that the longer part of the towel hangs down below if you were to hold it up by the handles.

* 5 *

To fold your beach bag up, lay it flat so that the pocket that you've sewed on is facing down. Fold the two sides of the towel inwards so it becomes the width of the pocket. Then fold the rest of the towel up from the bottom, making sure the folds are the same size as the pocket. Secure it all in place by turning your bag inside out.

* 6 *

Finished: you're ready to head to the beach.

MAKE
———— A HALTER-NECK ————
BIKINI OUT OF A T-SHIRT

If you're after a new bikini but don't fancy paying shop prices for such a teensy-weensy piece of material, then have a go at making one yourself. The measurements given are for a size 10. To go bigger, simply increase the measurements by holding it against yourself to resize.

* 1 *

Find two large t-shirts, choosing colours that work together.

* 2 *

Cut off two 3cm wide loops of material from the bottom of each of the T-shirts. Cut three of these in half to make six equal-sized strips and then cut the other one to make one longer strip.

* 3 *

To make the bikini top, cut a 25cm strip off one of the T-shirts. From this, cut out two triangles that measure 25cm along the bottom and 22cm on each side.

* 4 *

Next, hem the two triangles together along the shorter edges (you need two layers of material to ensure it doesn't go see-through) and turn your creation inside out. Then fold up the bottom side and sew in place to create a tunnel for your strap to be threaded through.

* 5 *

To finish the top, pull hard on your strips of material so they are lengthened and curl over. Then thread your longer piece through the triangle tunnel and sew two of the other pieces at the top to make the halter-neck straps.

* 6 *

To make the bottom, cut out two hourglass shapes that are 40cm long and measure 10 cm at the narrowest part. Hem this all around leaving one of the ends open to turn it inside out and then hem this side down as well.

* 7 *

Finish your bikini off by fixing the four remaining strips of material to the four corners of the hourglass so the bikini can be tied firmly in place.

MAKE A
—— PICNIC BLANKET ——
BOARD GAME

Not many people fancy lugging their board games around with them for some entertainment in the sun. To solve this little quandary you can make yourself a picnic blanket board game with the clever use of some good old-fashioned bleach.

Get hold of an old, dark, ideally single-coloured picnic blanket. Use some thick cardboard to make a backgammon or chess board stencil. Next, position your stencil onto your picnic mat (I went for the centre) and carefully spray it with a 50:50 bleach and water solution that you've made up in a household spray bottle. Be very careful not to get this solution anywhere else on the rug or on yourself. Instant gratification: your rug is finished!

MAKE A
—— PADDED PICNIC ——
BLANKET

Stand out from the crowd with this really simple and easy to make picnic blanket. Cut two large pieces of old curtain material (or some thick fabric of your choice – I use old curtain material a lot!) to your preferred size (I went for 3m by 3m), making sure one of them is 3cm bigger all round. You'll now need a piece of wadding that is the same size as your smaller piece of material. Make a wadding sandwich with the material on either side and then wrap the larger piece over the edges of the wadding and pin it onto the bottom piece, ensuring that it's also hemmed over. Don't forget to fold your corners in for a neat finish. Sew all around your edges and you're done. If you can't find bits of material or wadding big enough, then join smaller pieces together; you'll also need to sew up and down and across the whole blanket (giving a quilted effect) to keep smaller bits of wadding in place.

—— MAKE A ——
SCARECROW

Every discerning gardener needs a scarecrow, but more often than not they're up to their armpits in compost and just don't have the time to make one. To answer their bird scaring prayers, follow this simple guide to making a scarecrow. For extra scaring authenticity you can even model it on them:

＊ 1 ＊

Cut a long branch or bamboo cane into two pieces, one shorter for the arms and one longer for the body.

＊ 2 ＊

Fix the two pieces together to create a cross by binding with twine or wire.

＊ 3 ＊

Next, the fun part – getting the scarecrow dressed. Place an old shirt on the arms and button up.

＊ 4 ＊

Pull a pair of trousers onto your upright and tie the bottom of each of the trouser legs. Stuff both the shirt and trousers with straw or dried leaves, and then tuck the shirt in before tying in place with a rope or belt.

* 5 *

Place a pair of marigolds or old gloves at the end of
the arms and secure them with rubber bands or string.

* 6 *

Make a head for your scarecrow by stuffing straw into a
pillowcase. Skewer it onto the top of the branch or
cane and secure with string.

* 7 *

Draw a face with felt-tip pens, or glue on buttons for
eyes and wool for a mouth. Finished! Stick it in the
middle of the recipient's vegetable garden early one
morning for a brilliant surprise.

—— MAKE A ——
SCARE-SPARROW

If your patch of Eden is more of a window box then you could
make a scare-sparrow instead. This miniature version of the real
thing adds a fantastic rustic and personal touch. Here's how:

* 1 *

Get two sticks (one longer than the other) and tie them
together in a cross.

* 2 *

Put an old baby grow on your stick cross so that the
shorter stick is poking out of either of the armholes.

One end of the longer stick should be in a leg, and the other should stick out of the neck hole.

* 3 *

Stuff the baby grow with straw or anything you can get your hands on (old plastic bags are also great), and tie up the arms and feet to prevent the stuffing falling out.

* 4 *

Make the head out of a paper bag, an old small pillowcase or a dishtowel that's seen better days. Draw the face on with felt tips or stick on buttons, felt or wool instead. Tie it securely in place with string and put a baby's bonnet on top for extra authenticity.

Summer afternoon – summer afternoon; to me those have always been the two most beautiful words in the English language.
Henry James

MAKE SUMMER BUNTING

Bunting is one of the simplest home-made projects and a fantastic way to add a colourful, warm and friendly touch to your summer garden:

* 1 *

Gather together lots of brightly coloured pieces of material. Hunt around charity shops for old bedspreads and curtains (or be inventive and use brightly coloured thick plastic).

* 2 *

Draw a triangle on a piece of card and use this as a template. Cut out triangle shapes from your material using pinking shears to save you hemming each piece.

* 3 *

Finally, take some relatively thick binding tape (about 3 cm is ideal), and pin your fabric triangles along it, mixing up your materials to create a colourful display. Sew these into place, ideally with a sewing machine, and hang up in your garden to enjoy.

Making A Splash

> *There is nothing – absolutely nothing –*
> *half so much worth doing as*
> *simply messing about in boats.*
> Kenneth Grahame, *The Wind in the Willows*

For some, the local swimming pool offers the most convenient escape from the muggy heat of summer, and in recent years, thanks to the work of campaigners, we have seen the return of the lido. These once naff leisure venues have now been updated and re-invented. There has also been a breakout movement to escape the caged boundaries of our swimming pools. Across the country, swimmers have been liberating themselves from chlorine-filled municipal pools and diving into open, flowing waters to set their swimming free.

This chapter will help you to discover the deliciousness of outdoor swimming, and will also describe some of the other energetic ways you can explore this country's waterways and have fun with water to escape the heat when the summer's sun is riding high.

THE RETURN OF THE LIDO

The lido had its heyday in the thirties when local councils built some 150 of them across the UK. Sadly, the arrival of the shiny, sunny package holiday reflected badly on these local pools and in the seventies and eighties they came to be seen as tired and tawdry. Many stunning art deco pools and buildings were closed by councils in response to dwindling interest. In recent years, though, we have seen the return of the lido across the country: cities such as Bristol, London and Cambridge have seen huge surges of interest and support for outdoor swimming pools. These once written-off leisure facilities are now becoming major attractions.

WILD SWIMMING

The nation's rekindled love of outdoor swimming can in large part be credited to Roger Deakin's book *Waterlog*, a tale of one swimmer's journey through the wild waters of Britain. The book has been a gentle driving force behind the resurgence of interest in exploring our wild rivers and lakes, the return of the lido and the opening of river swimming clubs up and down the country. We have seen MPs campaigning for an increase in the number of outdoor bathing locations, and campaigns to change Welsh legislation to allow free access to waterways (to bring Wales in line with the rest of the UK).

Outdoor swimming as a leisure pursuit emerged during the 19th century when the romantic movement saw artists, poets and writers celebrate it as a way to commune with nature. Wordsworth is said to have enjoyed a cooling dip in the murky waters of the Lake District and later in the century a pre-breakfast swim was celebrated in Jerome K. Jerome's book, *Three Men in a Boat*. From here, wild swimming moved from the eccentric indulgence of artists to a leisure pursuit enjoyed by all. In the twenties over 600 river swimming clubs opened across the UK, and the pursuit became a regular part of physical education in schools across the country.

If you fancy giving wild swimming a go, then the best place to start is the Outdoor Swimming Society's website: www.outdoorswimmingsociety.com. It's a brilliant source of information and is full of useful stuff such as safety advice, information on events and a guide to the best wild swimming spots across the UK. To help you get started, the OSS team has kindly provided the following tips and techniques to get the most out of your wild swim :

Outdoor swimming technique: when it comes to technique, the key thing any wild swimmer should learn is exhaling under water. The most common reason for running out of oxygen while swimming is because you haven't exhaled fully, which leaves you gasping for breath. Practise breathing to both sides (bi-lateral breathing). Breathing every third stroke (to either side) is more efficient than breathing every second stroke, and means you can breathe away from wind and waves if necessary. It's also important to learn to breathe above the chop, so you don't inhale mouthfuls of water. Your outstretched arm with palm flat in the water helps provide a pivoting point as you inhale: simply rotate your chin further from the surface of the water before you breathe in.

Keep your eyes on what's ahead: a vital part of the outdoor swimmers stroke is the 'spot'. Where you look up to see where you're going. Spotting is simple in breaststroke, which is one of the reasons it is a popular stroke in recreational open water swimming. To spot in front crawl, take a breath and then on the next stroke simply look up as your forward arm enters the water and begins pulling down. You needn't raise your whole head out of the water, and don't breathe on this stroke as your throat will be constricted. Simply look up enough so you can see, then lower your head and complete the stroke. Breathe on the next stroke.

* * *

Get yourself a wetsuit: feeling the touch of the river or lake on your skin is one of the intoxicating delights of wild swimming. If however you're planning on taking things further than the occasional dip then a wetsuit becomes essential. The wetsuit isn't just about keeping you warm. It's also a key safety device as it helps with your buoyancy, allows you to stay in the water longer and enables you to swim faster and further as it cuts out the drag on your skin. You can either hire or buy your wetsuit, but make sure you research it properly – the difference between a £100 suit and a £150 suit can be huge.

* * *

Be safe by being seen: even if you eschew all swimming gear and take the plunge in your pants, you still need a brightly coloured silicone hat to ensure you're seen and to provide extra (and often essential) warmth. A bright colour makes you visible to other swimmers, and boat traffic. I've seen many a near miss where boats speed past our houseboat totally unaware of the naked headed swimmer in the water. Darkened wet hair means boats are almost certainly unable to see you. Avoid any colour seen in nature – black, blue, greens, white or silver, and go for something bright. You can get hold of a silicone hat from sports shop or the OSS online shop (www.outdoorswimmingsociety.com).

MIDNIGHT
SKINNY-DIPPING

Next time you go on holiday or are close to the sea, a lake or river, then please be tempted to do one thing: when the sun has set and all the beachcombers, fishermen, sunbathers and surfers have headed home, take your clothes off and slip into the dark water for a naked midnight swim. There is no feeling more liberating than that of wild water as it streams free across your body. Pop it on your 'things to do before I die' list and make sure it's ticked off before long.

RIVER BUGGING

River bugging was invented in New Zealand and essentially involves strapping yourself into an inflatable armchair and throwing yourself down white-water rapids. The single-person craft sends the rider (or 'bugger') winging their way down the river. As it's a fairly new sport, there are only a few dozen places in Europe where you can give it a go, but around half of them are in Scotland. Go online to find providers, and do not try it on your own in an unregulated environment.

GORGE WALKING

Gorge walking gives a whole new edge to a Sunday stroll by the river. The aim is to follow a river on its course as it dives through deep gorges and glides through mountainous landscapes. It can involve climbing beside waterfalls, sliding down rapids, floating down fast-flowing chutes and clinging onto rock faces. Wales has some of the best natural formations for gorge walking in the world. Search online for gorge walking possibilities.

CANYONING AND COASTEERING

Canyoning is the big brother of gorge walking. In this adrenalin-charged activity, you follow the course of a river and throw yourself off whatever waterfall impedes your progress and swim through caves that cut through the mountains. Coasteering is the saltwater cousin of canyoning and involves navigating your way along the coastline by rock climbing, cliff jumping and swimming. It takes a brave adventurer, but the adrenalin rushes are worth it. You can find centres offering both sports all over the UK.

STREAM SPRINTING
AND
RIVER RUNNING

If canyoning and coasteering sound a bit too ambitious for you, then why not start out with a spot of homespun river running instead. When you're next taking a walk along a gently wandering stream or river, then this is a great challenge: it's one that I've indulged since my teenage years. The idea is to see how far you can get along the river by balancing on the banks and bouncing across protruding rocks without getting your feet wet. If you fancy diving in, then it's a race to see how far you can follow the river without getting out – we used to compete in a peaty Dartmoor river, scrambling over its mossy underwater boulders to see who could be the first up from the valley to the top of the waterfall. This activity, as you might imagine, comes with all the necessary warnings: be safe and only choose gentle, meandering rivers that you know well.

BUILD A RIVER RAFT

If you fancy going all Huckleberry Finn, then have a go at building your own river raft. Here are a few tips to ensure your raft doesn't sink as soon as you get on-board:

✴ 1 ✴

Gather some long branches or logs if you can find
them, and cut off any protruding twigs. Create your
punting pole by choosing a long, straight and smooth
branch. You'll need to test the deepest part of your
river with your punt stick to ensure it's going to be of
any use.

✴ 2 ✴

Lay the rest of the branches on the ground beside each
other. Using some thin rope or strong string, bind the
branches or logs together at each end, using a sort of
weaving technique.

✴ 3 ✴

Once both ends are securely bound, test your raft's
buoyancy and, if you're happy, jump on-board and set
sail.

——— MAKE A ROPE ———
SWING

Rope swings are always a sign of a river that's well used and loved
by kids. The rope swing that hung over the river near my aunt's
house in Devon had to be replaced each year because of excessive
summertime use. The first teenager who leaps from the one that
hangs near our houseboat provides a sign of the start of a long
summer of riverside fun.

To make a rope swing you need to have a sturdy rope and a strong piece of smooth wood – but more importantly you need a deep enough pool that is free of any sort of obstruction and has a really strong branch hanging over it. It's hugely important that you test these things and it must be done by an adult.

To set up the swing, measure the rope out so it's the right length to enable the kids to get on from the bank when it's hung in the tree, taking into consideration the extra length needed to secure it in place. Tie a strong loop in one end of the rope and then securely knot the piece of wood to the other end. Next, you need to climb the tree and attach the rope to the branch by poking the wooden end through the loop, and feeding it down so that it's suspended over the pool of water. Make sure you test it a couple of times before letting the kids have a go.

RIVER DAYS OUT

Rivers are like pathways that cut through the land to lead you to otherwise inaccessible parts of our country. They are the uncelebrated back routes through cities and corridors into the countryside that allow you to see so much more. Before I moved in to a houseboat, I spent months hiring boats and kayaks to explore the waterways around Greater London. They were like channels of fresh air within the city, allowing me to explore a huge variety of suburban secrets. There are lots of ways to discover our country's waterways, from organised boat tours to heading off under your own steam. Whether it's by kayak, canoe, river raft or motorboat, a short search on the Internet will lead you to a wealth of suppliers to get you on-board and on your way. Plan your route, ideally with a destination to head for. Pack your waterproofs and a picnic and set out. It really is as easy as that.

GO CANOEING

Canoeing is a perfect way to explore the UK's waterways. If you can swim and grasp the navigation of a craft by paddle then you're set to give it a go. It's also a relatively cheap sport to partake in. The best place to get started is to become a member of your local canoe club. Club subscriptions vary depending on where you are in the country and you can find all the information you need by visiting the British Canoe Union at www.bcu.org.uk.

GO PADDLEBOARDING

Some of the more unusual river regulars on my home stretch of the Thames are the paddleboarders. I first saw one late one summer's evening; we hadn't been living on the river long and were still intoxicated by the delight of life on the water. I'd just got back from work and was cooking supper in the kitchen, gazing dreamily at the river, when I caught sight of Christ's second coming. A man was walking on water, quite literally gliding past the window. A closer look revealed an ordinary fellow standing on an elongated surfboard and propelling himself along with a long-handled, single-bladed paddle. His arrival on the river was soon to set a trend. By the following spring, we were regularly treated to the sight of paddleboarders skimming past our home.

Paddleboarding is proving to be a hip way to exercise and has many celebrity followers, including Jennifer Aniston. It claims to do you more good in thirty minutes than several hours' worth of surfing. In fact, Americans have got so into it that paddleboard yoga has taken off. The thought of people doing headstands on surfboards is a little mind-boggling. If you fancy giving more conventional paddleboarding a go then here are some possibilities around the UK. A lot of these are based on the coast, but many also offer the opportunity to explore calmer inland waterways:

> The Fen Paddle Company (www.fenpaddle.co.uk)
> offers a fantastic way to explore the fens of East Anglia.
>
> * * *
>
> The Blue Chip Surf shop in Cheam, Surrey, supplies
> kit and run courses if you fancy having a go on the Thames.

* * *

Try Harlyn Surf School in Cornwall (www.harlynsurfschool.co.uk) if the aqua blue waters of the southwest coast are a little more alluring.

* * *

Adventure Sports Holidays (www.adventuresportsholidays.com) have a great selection of trips and courses across the UK.

* * *

If you're in Bournemouth or Poole then head to www.coastwiththemost.com for a list of local paddleboarding outfits.

* * *

For Brighton-based adventures, visit www.thebrightonwatersports.co.uk for introductory courses and kit.

* * *

Further North, try www.boardskillz.co.uk for the Tyne, Tees and Lake District areas.

* * *

In Whitby, contact the East Barnby Outdoor Education Centre (www.outdoored.co.uk/EastBarnby/).

* * *

If you're in Yorkshire try the Fluid Concept Surf Shop in Scarborough (www.fluidconcept.co.uk).

* * *

In Ireland there's Jamie Knox, based in County Kerry (www.jamieknox.com).

* * *

In North Wales give www.sunsetclub.co.uk a go.

HAVE A
—— SPLASHING ——
TIME IN THE GARDEN

If all of that sounds a little too far from the comforts of home, then there are some simpler and more old-fashioned ways to keep cool in your garden:

Make a waterslide by spreading a large plastic sheet on your lawn and running a hose down it, along with a healthy squirt of washing up liquid. When you're ready, throw yourself down it.

* * *

Hold a water-bomb war (see page 89).

* * *

Turn your garden pond into a swimming pool (see page 96).

* * *

Finally, an old childhood favourite: turn the sprinkler on and throw some shapes as you jump through it.

Let your boat of life be light, packed with only what you need — a homely home and simple pleasures, one or two friends, worth the name, someone to love and someone to love you, a cat, a dog, and a pipe or two, enough to eat and enough to wear, and a little more than enough to drink; for thirst is a dangerous thing.

Jerome K. Jerome, *Three Men in a Boat*

How Refreshing

When it comes to quenching your thirst on a hot day, then our summer season offers a stack of home-grown and exotic choices that have the power to transport you to another place. If the day is looking overcast, one of my favourite ways to escape to the sun is to cut open a passion fruit and breathe in the rich tropical scent of the Caribbean. The sweet-and-sour tang of fresh Jamaican limeade has a similar effect.

Any discussion of summer drinks wouldn't be complete without touching on the season's favourite alcoholic tipples. Think of cocktails and cool, crisp wines: summer wouldn't be the same without an afternoon spent celebrating the sun with a fruit-laden Pimms in hand. There are certain drinks that can only be enjoyed properly at the right time of year. Sipping a glass of sangria when the trees are without their leaves will leave you seriously discombobulated. But as soon as it's warm enough to bare your arms and legs, then it's open season on summer's delicious tipples.

This chapter describes how to make some of the most deliciously thirst-quenching summer drinks. There are those that you can pick and brew by hand, others that require a juicer or kitchen blender and a couple that merely require you to nip to your local shop to arm yourself with the ingredients. Hopefully, your future taste of summer will be found right here.

LASHINGS OF
——— HOME-MADE ———
GINGER BEER

This is a real summer classic, and the favoured tipple of the Famous Five when celebrating having solved another mystery. It only takes about half an hour to mix together and a couple of days to ferment.

Ingredients

1 tbsp fresh ginger, finely chopped

1 unwaxed lemon, thickly sliced

250g golden caster sugar

½ tsp cream of tartar (available at large supermarkets or health stores)

¾ tsp dried fast-action yeast (as above)

1. Mix the ginger, lemon, sugar and cream of tartar with 750ml of cold water in a large pan. Cover and slowly bring to the boil, stirring all the time to dissolve the sugar. As soon as it starts to boil, reduce the heat and then simmer for 5 minutes. Next, add 1.5l of cold water and sprinkle over the yeast. Cover again and set aside in a cool place overnight.

2. The next step is to sterilise two 1.5l bottles. I always sterilise my bottles in the dishwasher, leaving them to fully steam dry before use. If you don't have a dishwasher then you can clean out glass bottles with boiling water before putting them in a low oven for 15 minutes to dry.

3. Strain all of the pieces out of the ginger beer and pour it into your two bottles, making sure there is a decent gap at the top to allow for the fermentation process to take place without the bottle exploding.

4. Leave in a cool, dark place for between 12 and 36 hours. Your ginger beer will be ready to drink as soon as it's fizzy. Make sure you finish it off within three days – leave it longer and it will start to go off.

ELDERFLOWER CORDIAL

The delightful elder bush, hobbit of suburban wastelands, city streets and country hedges, goes into full bloom at the end of spring and start of summer. The best time to pick the flowers is in the morning when the sun is out in full force and the bushes have just burst into flower, as this is when the smell and flavour is at its finest. Avoid any with a darker or brown colour as these can turn your cordial foul. Cut the flower heads as close to the stems as possible using scissors, and make sure you have as little stem as possible in your harvest. Gently shake each flower-head after picking to remove any insects who might be enjoying their breakfast. This is our family recipe for elderflower cordial, one that has been tried and tested for three generations:

Ingredients
1.5l boiling water
1kg white granulated sugar
20 large elderflower heads in the first flush of full bloom
4 lemons
55ml citric acid (this helps to preserve your cordial)

1. Take a large, scrupulously clean bowl, bucket or saucepan and stir the sugar into the boiling water until fully dissolved.

2. Leave to cool and then add the citric acid, the juice and zest of the lemons and the elderflower heads. Stir this gently and then leave to steep for 48 hours.

3. Then strain your mixture through a clean muslin cloth into a jug, and use a funnel to pour it into sterilised bottles (see the ginger beer recipe on page 126 for sterilising instructions).

4. Once bottled, seal and store. If you used the citric acid, your cordial will keep for four months in the fridge. I often make a second batch in plastic bottles for the freezer to keep myself stocked up right through to the next season.

ELDERFLOWER CHAMPAGNE

I was brought up on elderflower champagne until my mother realised that it contained alcohol! A minimal amount, but noticeable when the children have consumed a litre each at a family christening. We've always made large volumes of the stuff, so the family recipe below is designed to produce about 11 litres. If you want half the quantity, then simply halve the ingredients. Follow the picking instructions described for the elderflower cordial to ensure the best flavour for your brew.

Ingredients
50 good-sized elderflower heads
3kg caster sugar
11 tbsp white wine vinegar
11l boiling water
11 large lemons

1. Put your 11 litres of boiling water in a scrupulously clean bucket, stir in the sugar until fully dissolved and leave to cool. Once ready, add the vinegar, the juice and zest from the lemons and then the flower heads, gently dunking them as you place each one in. Give it one final stir before leaving to stand in a cool, dark place for 72 hours with a large muslin cloth or tea towel over the top.

2. Now is the crucial time: the trick when making elderflower champagne is to ensure that your mixture starts to ferment rather than go off. If the fermentation

process hasn't started after two days then add a small pinch of brewer's yeast to get things moving. Bubbles on the top of the mixture are an indication that your champagne is fermenting. If you notice any mould, that's a sign that the sugar isn't going to ferment and unfortunately you'll need to throw your mixture away and start again.

3. After leaving it for 72 hours, strain the liquid through a clean muslin cloth and pour it into sterilised bottles (see the ginger beer recipe for sterilising instructions). As bottles of elderflower champagne have been known to explode, it's important that you avoid cork bottles. If you want to play it super safe then use screw-top plastic bottles and release a small amount of the pressure once a week. I've always used recycled swing-top Grolsch bottles and have never had a problem.

ROSE HIP SYRUP

One of the little-sung tastes of summer is the rose bush. Their brightly coloured flowers are celebrated around the world, but it's only in a few countries such as Turkey that the taste is experienced widely. I adore adding the taste of rose to summer drinks by using this syrup to create a rose martini. Alternatively, use it to make a refreshing cordial by adding to sparkling water. It's also particularly delicious on my morning porridge. Unfortunately, my love isn't shared by all: during World War II, rose hip syrup became a key source of vitamin C for nutrient-starved city dwellers. School children would be sent out on foraging excursions to collect vast quantities of rose hips for the mass production of syrup. Because of the daily medicinal dose the children were forced to take, my rose hip syrup can elicit 'yuck' noises from the older generations. But if you fancy a refreshing change from supermarket fruit cordials then follow this simple recipe:

Ingredients
1 kg rose hips, washed and roughly chopped
1 kg caster sugar

1. Throw the chopped rose hips into 2l of boiling water and bring back to the boil. Then remove from the heat, cover and leave to infuse for half an hour, stirring from time to time.

2. Strain the mixture through a sterilised jelly bag. Alternatively, line a colander with a couple of layers of sterilised muslin and place over a large bowl or pan. Tip in the rose hip mixture, and leave to strain through overnight.

3. Set the strained juice aside and transfer the rose hip pulp back to the saucepan, along with another litre of boiling water. Bring to the boil, remove from the heat, infuse for another half an hour and strain as before. Discard the pulp and combine the two lots of strained juice in a clean pan. Boil until the volume has decreased by half, then remove from the heat.

4. Add the sugar, return to the stove and stir until dissolved. Boil hard for five minutes, then pour into warmed, sterilised jars or bottles and seal. The syrup should be kept in the fridge and used within three months.

——— JERRY'S JAMAICAN ——— LIMEADE

There is nothing like a glass of cold limeade to cut through the fug of a humid summer day. Our friend Jerry in Jamaica used to make a beautiful jug of the stuff that would settle us in back home after a hard day at the beach. Don't tell everyone, but he said I could feature his secret recipe here:

Ingredients
6 good-sized limes
100g brown sugar
1.25l water

Juice your limes, saving a couple of slices for garnish. Add the brown sugar (you can add more or less than specified to taste) to the juice along with a little of the water and stir until the sugar is dissolved. Tip the mixture into a big jug full of ice and pour in the rest of the water.

THE BEST SMOOTHIES AND JUICES

When it was realised that you could get your five a day in a glass before you'd even stepped in the shower, people started to order fruit in bulk. Sadly it was a short-lived fad, probably largely due to the frustrating task of cleaning the machines. As a result, abandoned juice machines can now be found up and down the country collecting dust at the back of kitchen cupboards, alongside pasta makers and lean mean grilling machines. But if we accepted the cleaning process in the same vein as doing the dishes then juicers really are a great way to get your day's nutrients in one hit.

I've listed a few smoothie recipes below, and featured ones that can be made with or without complicated juicing machines and the resulting cleaning chores!

TROPICAL TREAT

This is a tropical classic and a real zinger of a way to start the day. It's best done in a juicer but can be made in a blender. If you choose the blender option, then you might want to strain it before drinking to get rid of any unblitzed fibres. To whizz one together, simply juice up a mango, a pineapple, a lime and 2cm of ginger root and pour into a glass over ice.

HAPPY JUICE

This one's great to give you an energy boost and is packed full of fantastic antioxidants thanks to the properties of the magical blueberry. Not only are they said to lower your risk of heart disease and cancer, but they also put you in a great mood too. To make your happy juice, simply blitz two passion fruit along with a mango, a pineapple and 150g of bluberries for one smile-making treat.

STRAIGHT UP BANANA SMOOTHIE

A breakfast favourite and a great way to give your body a healthy kick-start to the day. To make one, simply slice two bananas into your food blender along with 250ml of milk and 250ml of yoghurt. If you want to keep things cool then pop an ice cube into the mix as well. You can also add honey to sweeten or half a vanilla pod for a great alternative flavour. Blitz up for a few seconds until the mixture runs smooth and Bob's your uncle.

WATERMELON CRUSH

A perfect accompaniment for a day spent lounging in the garden. Blast a quarter of a watermelon, 10 strawberries and the juice of one lime along with some ice in a blender, adding a touch of honey if you fancy it.

SOME SUMMER DRINKS TIPS

Fruit ice cubes

If all the above sounds like too much work then a great way to add a touch of sun to your drinks is to freeze summer fruit in ice cubes. Ice-bound raspberries and curls of lemon rind add a fantastic touch of colour to jugs of water, or put ice-cubed mint leaves and orange slices in Pimms for an alternative to the usual fruit mix.

Frozen slices of lemon

This is a great tip from my aunt: by freezing slices of lemon, they double up as ice cubes and are also a great way to use up lemons if they're starting to dry up at the bottom of your fruit bowl.

Pastry cutter shapes

Use pastry cutters to cut out interesting shapes from hard fruits such as apples and melons and put these into or onto the side of the glass for a brilliant decorative effect.

Be creative with your stirrers

Slices of cucumber, mint stalks and celery make great cocktail stirrers as well as adding another layer of flavour to drinks. Cucumber goes well with gin, celery with vodka and mint with all sorts including lemonade and the classic glass of Pimms.

A Home-Grown Summer

> *The man who has planted a garden feels that he has done something for the good of the world.*
> Vita Sackville-West

The past few years have heard the low murmur of a gardening revolution. A growing movement of individuals who would have previously baulked at the idea of getting mud on their manicured talons or putting their well-heeled toes into wellies are now doing so with relish. The numbers jumping on the 'grow-your-own' express have turned Britain from a nation of shopkeepers to a nation of gardeners instead. Urban wastelands are being used to nurture tomatoes, rose beds are being dug up to house brassicas, and the waiting list to get an allotment makes getting tickets for Glastonbury look easy.

If you've never had a go at growing your own food then it really will be a summer activity that opens the doors to new levels of pleasure. It's something that anyone can try – whether you have a sunny windowsill or a herbaceous border ripe for conversion into a raised vegetable bed. To provide you with a guide to what to grow throughout the summer, I have called on the help and advice of my uncle Ronald, gardening fanatic and vegetable-growing supremo.

Ronald is an evangelist when it comes to home growing. His love of nurturing vegetables goes back to the war when as a little boy he helped his great aunts 'Dig for Victory' on their allotment. If you've never felt the heart-warming benefits of growing and eating your own food, then you certainly should follow Ronald's advice on ten vegetables for the summer months.

The vegetables chosen for this chapter are particularly suitable for beginners who are either growing at home or making a start on an allotment. In case outdoor space is limited, Ronald has also advised on a few options that are ideal for growing in pots and tubs. Given the size and complexity of the subject, this chapter is written to inspire the beginner to give home growing a go. If you are bitten by the bug, then take your reading further and wider. There is a wealth of expert books out there to help you grow your knowledge.

TEN
VEGETABLES FOR
THE BEGINNER'S GARDEN

I have always been a bit miffed at the perfection of vegetables found on supermarket shelves. They appear so faultless that I've often questioned whether machines make them. My carrots more closely resemble gargoyles than the cone-shaped orange soldiers that are bagged up in shops. But it's when you come to the taste test that the truth comes out. The bland taste of a sprayed, spruced, plastic-bagged carrot that has been hanging about in a warehouse for weeks is incomparable to the deep, fresh crunch and earthy taste of one of my gargoyles that has been pulled fresh from the ground. They are untouched by chemicals, and it is much reported that vegetables picked and eaten within 30 minutes hold on to more of their vitamins and minerals, making them much better for you.

After many long conversations and extensive family debate, Ronald has selected 10 vegetables for this chapter whose taste far exceeds that of those that you can purchase in the supermarket. An obvious omission is garden peas. They didn't make the final cut as the frozen ones are so delicious and sweet; they are processed very soon after picking and are one of the few things that are usually better frozen. They are also rather hard work to grow in quantities decent enough to satisfy the family. The pigeons also love them leaving even less for you.

So here you have it – Uncle Ronald's advice on 10 vegetables that are ideal for the beginner vegetable grower. I hope you find something here to inspire you to don your gardening gloves and embrace the compost.

JUNE
Early June marks the end of the 'hungry gap'. In days gone by, May was the time when the larder finally lay bare after a long winter of eking out the stores. It was a time when hunger would set in and everyone looked forward to the fruits of the growing season. The hawthorn was one of the first small trees to return to green during these late spring months, and their leaves were called 'bread and cheese' as hungry children would eat them. The dance around the maypole marked the start of a new season of plenty and was a celebration to welcome the return of the summer

months. These days, as our food is flown in daily from warmer climes, the 'hungry gap' has become a thing of the past. But June can still be a time to enjoy early planted broad beans, the fresh green taste of newly picked asparagus spears dipped in lemony butter, and the sharp sweet pudding treat of rhubarb. You could also try for some early potatoes.

Broad beans

Vegetable gardening can be a highly competitive activity. Each year Ronald and his sister Penny are in competition to see who can be the first to serve home-grown broad beans with the Sunday roast. Penny's clever tactic of sowing hers before the winter's frosts set in, usually positions her as the forerunner. So save yourself some spring work and get your beans in during autumn.

When to plant: If you are brave, you can plant in October or early November. It is safer to plant your seeds in 12cm pots (12 to a pot) in mid-February, keeping them covered with fleece and planting out in mid- to late March. This is my technique, as in Devon where I live the rooks would think Christmas had come if they spied the earliest delicate shoots.

Pests and preventatives: The black fly loves to gorge on broad beans when the tender top leaves have reached their peak. Tackle this threat by picking the young leaves and cooking them in the same way as you would baby spinach for a delicious late spring treat.

How to look after them: Your plants may become rather tall, so have some canes and twine ready to hold them up.

When to pick: Pick as soon as the beans are formed in the pods. Don't leave them for too long as the beans toughen and lose their fantastic fresh texture and taste.

Asparagus

Asparagus is an iconic status symbol to have growing in your garden. Beyond the taste, it also has all sorts of health benefits. The famous French herbalist Maurice Mességué claimed asparagus calms palpitations and is ideal for people under stress. It was the Romans who first bought the seeds to Britain. They collected them from Egypt where the ancients believed that the spears grew from rams' horns buried in the soil. The one frustrating factor that any gardener has to wrangle with is that it takes about two years from planting before the fruits of your labour can be enjoyed. It is, however, worth waiting for. Fresh from the garden, there is no comparison with stale ones from the shop or soggy spears in tins.

When to plant: Buy 2- to 3-year-old 'crowns' and plant in April. This is a cheat's method to avoid the long wait for seeds to turn into spears.

How to look after them: Cover with compost. Cut down the ferny stems in the autumn when they turn yellow.

When to pick: At the earliest in May. The main cut will be in early June.

Rhubarb

Although it is possible to grow rhubarb from seed, it is much easier and more reliable to grow it from a crown. The area around a rhubarb plant cannot be dug once the plant is established as this can damage the roots, therefore sufficient space needs to be left around it. Ronald's recipe recommendation is to bake them in the oven with fresh orange zest and some crystallised ginger.

When to plant: Buy crowns at the end of winter and plant in March ready to pick in the following year. My favourite rhubarb variety is the 'Timperley Early', which is a renowned early variety.

How to look after them: Plant straight into the ground in a hole a little wider than the plant, so that the top of the crown is around 3cm below the surface. Mulch around the plant, but not directly over the top of the crown. Rhubarb grows best in a sunny position, although it will tolerate some shade. It prefers neutral soil dug to at least half a metre with as much fertilising organic matter (well-rotted manure or compost) forked in as possible. It will also thrive in a large pot.

When to pick: Pull the sticks when the leaves are fully formed. Discard the leaves, which are poisonous.

Early potatoes

Another competitive challenge for June is to get an early crop of potatoes. Last year both Ronald's and mine were nipped by those dreaded late May frosts. The key to getting a good early crop is to choose 'First Earlies', the variety that is most likely to deliver the much-anticipated first potatoes of the year.

When to plant: Plant in mid-March, though you will always be at risk from ruination by late frosts. The trick is to buy seed potatoes early. Place them in trays with a base of peat (or similar). They will then shoot and should be planted carefully in the ground with the shoots uppermost. This is called 'chitting' and it's vital for early potatoes. Potatoes can also be grown in large buckets or containers. I grow mine on my balcony in an old chest I picked up from a junkyard.

Pests and preventatives: If it's wet and warm the dreaded potato blight may strike. Its spores will land on your potato leaves, enter the plants via tiny pores (called stomata), and then feast on the plant and multiply. It usually strikes in early June, so a successful early crop is a vegetable gardener's triumph.

When to pick: Dig up and enjoy at the end of June.

JULY

Now we come to July, a season of mellow fruitfulness. This is the time to keep busy with the hoe to defeat the weeds. Slugs and snails are also a major menace. Ronald's deterrent is a pet Muscovy Duck called Mr Sealing Wax because of his red wax-like beak, but sadly for the rest of us it's more like beer traps or other, non-organic approaches.

Courgettes

For some reason marrows have gone out of favour. If, like Ronald, you remain a fan then the trick is to grow what are now fashionably called 'courgettes'. These are merely marrows picked young. Ronald is always secretly delighted when he is caught out and a courgette, which has been hidden under a large leaf, turns into a massive marrow. According to Marrow Master Ronald, stuff and bake with seasoned mince and see if that doesn't convert the sceptics. My favourite courgette dish is to slice them and fry them in lots of butter until lightly browned. Simple perfection.

When to plant: To ensure an early crop, plant two seeds per small pot in early May and keep warm. Plant out seedlings when the risks of frost are over. In frost-prone areas it would be advisable to wait until the end of the legendary 'Franklin Nights', in the latter part of May, are over.

How to look after them: Plant on a mound of soil and cover with mulch (old newspapers or rotten leaves are both ideal) to retain moisture.

When to pick: This ubiquitous vegetable keeps on delivering throughout the season.

Salad Leaves

Responding to the growing interest in freshly picked salad leaves, there are now superb seed offerings of lettuce varieties with colour, texture and flavour. A good way to start is to choose a packet of 'Gourmet Mixed' seeds. The herbalist Mességué describes the lettuce as 'the herb of wisdom' and it is also supposed to cure insomnia, act as a sedative, and have anti-aphrodisiacal properties. There are many tantalising varieties of salad leaves both spicy and mild. You could try 'Mixed Spicy Salad Leaves' for a tangy and peppery result.

When to plant: End of March onwards.

What to plant in: Salad leaves can be grown very successfully in containers and this also helps to keep the slugs at bay. I get hold of old wooden vegetable trays from the greengrocer, lines them with old hessian sacks or newspaper, fills them with compost and plants different varieties in each one.

Picking: The plant will need to grow for 35 days or more before it's ready to pick. A good approach is to carefully harvest the middle leaves, leaving the outer and centre leaves in place. This allows the plant to grow on for the next picking.

Carrots

Carrots are always hugely popular with the family as well as with the gathering of pests who hover around the vegetable garden. To attempt the same tapered perfection as is found in supermarket specimens, sow them in pots and when they are 5cm high plant them in the ground. To do this, make a hole with a dibber, fill with compost and try and feed the root down straight into the hole. Though I have to say kids rather like my gargoyle friends.

When to plant: Sow in May for July.

Pests and preventatives: The clever carrot fly has an amazing ability to find every carrot crop in the country and will try to damage each one with black rings and holes. Ronald's top tip is to watch out for cow parsley in the hedgerows. Once it comes into flower then the carrot fly will soon arrive. Cover your carrots with fleece and keep them covered until the cow parsley has died down.

AUGUST

In August you need to prepare for watering, although a good way to minimise the task is to mulch crops with straw or old newspapers, which will retain what moisture there is. The autumn crops chosen here should make a good show. You can reflect on your first year's results and plan for the next while sitting out in the sunshine.

Runner beans

A row of runner beans can form a dense, attractive screen and a bean-covered wigwam can make a coloured focal point for the garden, as well as being delightful treat for the honeybee. Be warned there are snags with runner beans: they are prolific and best picked every day and then someone has to be persuaded to 'string' them. If they are left, they become tough and the fresh taste disappears, making them a candidate for the 'I dunner like it' collection. Ronald told me of a solution: a friend's son refused to eat runner beans but loved pasta. His mother strung the beans into long thin threads and served them as green spaghetti. The result? 'This is delicious'! Try it for yourself.

When to plant: From the end of May, after the last frost, and in succession so the pods don't all come at once. Sow a few extra at the end of each row to lift and fill any gaps.

When to pick: August to September.

Squash

Ronald has a squash 'arch' which marks the doorway to his impressive vegetable garden. Guests admire the sculptural feat of training these alien-like plants into such apparently complicit behaviour. If you are diligent in early sowing then you should be able to get a good crop of squashes in August. Select a variety that is good for eating when it is quite small and leave some to turn into fine Halloween pumpkins. They come in all sizes, shapes and colours, and many of them can be stored for several months through the winter.

When to plant: At the end of May. Plant two seeds per small pot, then plant out in mid-June.

How to look after them: Squash enjoy a good liquid fertiliser feed. Keep the roots moist.

Sweetcorn

The last of Ronald's chosen ten vegetables is usually a great favourite. A native of America, maize (a variety of which we know as sweetcorn) has become a staple around the world, particularly in African countries as it is relatively resistant to dry conditions.

The garden varieties are very sweet, but, once picked, the sugars in the kernels very quickly turn to starch. So the rule is to pick them no more than an hour before cooking. This beats all those perfect-looking ones in the shop. Be warned that, depending on where you live, there might be strong competition from badgers.

When to plant: To defeat the slugs, plant your corn seeds in pots or tubes (old toilet rolls are ideal). Plant them out in June.

How to look after them: Sweetcorn must be grown in rectangular blocks and not in rows – this is to ensure wind pollination.

* * *

So there you have it, a basic beginner's guide to summer vegetables. I hope you will become an enthusiastic vegetable gardener and will pass your knowledge on to your friends, family, children and grandchildren. There are so many wonderful books with further advice from great gardeners like Geoff Hamilton and Alan Titchmarsh. Ronald let me into his secret: he always has on him a copy of the famous Dr Hessayon's *The Vegetable & Herb Expert* and Joy Larkcom's *Grow Your Own Vegetables.* He strongly recommends them. If everyone is impressed with the harvest from your first year of vegetable gardening, this will be the time to put in a bid for a small greenhouse so next year you can grow those luscious tomatoes that they complained were missing.

LAST DAYS OF SUMMER

'Tis the last rose of summer
Left blooming alone;
All her lovely companions
Are faded and gone;
No flower of her kindred,
No rosebud is nigh,
To reflect back her blushes,
To give sigh for sigh.
Thomas Moore, 'The Last Rose of Summer'

Last days of summer
must-do dates

AUGUST

✻

Notting Hill Carnival – a steel-drumming, reggae-dancing, sequin-shaking celebration of community solidarity

✻

SEPTEMBER

✻

Bestival – a hedonistic house party in a field on Isle of Wight

✻

The Great River Race – London's rowing marathon

✻

Bognor Regis Seaside Festival – triple servings of all that the British beach has to offer

✻

World Gurning Championship – held at the Egremont Crab Fair in Cumbria

✻

World Black Pudding Throwing Championships – Lancashire

✻

World Gravy Wrestling Championships – Lancashire

✻

The Last Night of the Proms – a festival of classical music in the Royal Albert Hall and Hyde Park

✻

Galway International Oyster Festival – if you like oysters, then this is your Arcadia

Whatever The Weather

> *How beautiful is the rain!*
> *After the dust and heat,*
> *In the broad and fiery street,*
> *In the narrow lane,*
> *How beautiful is the rain!*
> Henry Wadsworth Longfellow, 'Rain in Summer'

Most summers on our sometimes not-so-fair isle will be peppered with healthy doses of rain. Not that I'm complaining: we wouldn't be blessed with such a verdant countryside without a little bad weather. It does, however, pose a problem if you're stuck inside with a gaggle of kids who are itching for entertainment, particularly if you're determined to not bow down to the electric lure of the television. For those without children it can also present a quandary, as there are only so many pubs you can visit, films you can watch and papers and books you can read on a total washout of a weekend. You also want to feel that you've achieved something with your precious time and haven't just let it get washed down the drain.

This chapter should help you out if your summer is looking more wet than sunny. It's packed full of novel ways to fill your time and I hope it will inspire you to find your way to making your own entertainment. A British summer just wouldn't be the same without some rainy days.

> *I do think that, of all the silly, irritating tomfoolishness*
> *by which we are plagued, this 'weather-forecast' fraud is*
> *about the most aggravating. It 'forecasts' precisely what*
> *happened yesterday or the day before, and precisely the*
> *opposite of what is going to happen today.*
> Jerome K. Jerome, *Three Men in a Boat*

PUT ON A PLAY

This is likely to produce deep groans from half your gathered
group, but it really is one of those activities that, if you give it a go,
has the potential to turn a washout into a truly memorable day.
First of all, decide on what play you're going to perform – the
Internet is stacked with scripts that you can print out, or else pop
along to your local bookshop and pick up something of your
choosing. It's best to not be too ambitious: you could perform one
act or even just a few scenes to start with. You can conjure up
costumes from your linen cupboard or the attic. You never know,
you might uncover talents you never knew you had.

—— INDOOR SPORTS DAY ——

If the weather has blighted your much-anticipated, sun-soaked Sunday on the golf course or your garden game of croquet, then don't resign yourself to slumping on the sofa bemoaning the inclement conditions. Show some British stoicism and have a sporting day at home instead:

Play boules on your carpet. If you don't have a set of boules then use fruit instead.

* * *

How about a game of skittles using water-filled plastic bottles?

* * *

Use your dining-room table as a table football pitch. All you need is a marble and some flicking fingers.

* * *

Have a go at piggyback jousting and see who is first to be knocked down.

* * *

Or you could try a game of darts using a watermelon with a drawn-on dartboard instead of the usual target, and barbecue skewers for darts.

HAVE A GAME OF TIGHT RACING

This is a very amusing game to both watch and play. To give it a go, get everyone into pairs and gather two piles of weird and wonderful portable objects from around your home, along with a pair of tights per team. Divide the items into two equal halves. On the word 'go', one half of each pair needs to put the tights on (over clothes is fine) while the other races to put all of the items down the tights at the same time. Once done, it's a race to the end of the room or some other designated point and back. First in is the winner.

OLD JUMPER PUPPET SHOW

This is a great way to give an old jumper a new lease of life. The idea is that, with a little bit of sewing and a spot of cutting and gluing, you can create your very own wearable puppet show. Here's how:

> Find an old jumper. As the main part of the jumper is going to be your backdrop, use the colour to decide what type of puppet show you're going to create. If it's blue, you might decide on a nautical or aerial scene. If it's black, a spooky Halloween play would be more suitable.

* * *

Next, you need to sew up the ends of the sleeves – easy peasy.

* * *

Now for the fun bit: use old material and bits and pieces from the recycle bin to create the detail of the scene for your play. If, for example, it's set at sea, you might use green pieces of material for seaweed and a piece of tinfoil shaped into a hook that's attached to some string to look like someone's fishing line. Sew or stick them all in place.

* * *

If you want a scene change, you can also do something different on the back of the jumper.

* * *

Finally, you need to create your characters – that's what the arms of the jumper are for. To get the feel of it, put the jumper on and tuck the sleeves into your hands to create a mouth.

* * *

Stick on eyes and then build up appropriate human or animal features. If it's a crab, for example, an old orange sock could make the body. You could cut out and sew on cardboard crab claws on either side. A great way to create a sea snail would be to turn a tissue box into a shell with a bit of clever cutting and gluing. You could then thread your hand through the tissue hole and out through another hole on the other side to represent the snail's head.

* * *

Once you're finished, let the play commence.

MAKE A STACK OF ——— PINWHEELS TO ——— DECORATE YOUR GARDEN

This is a really simple craft activity that creates wonderfully colourful decorations for your garden, ready for when the sun comes out. Here's how to make them:

Take two coloured pieces of A4 paper, stick them back-to-back and then make a square by folding them into a triangle and cutting off the excess.

* * *

Next, fold your square into a small triangle by folding it in half (along the existing crease) and in half again.

* * *

Unfold it and cut along the fold marks until you are about 2cm from the middle and then fold down alternate flaps into the middle, ensuring that you leave the folds unpressed, to enable them to catch the wind.

* * *

Fix the flaps into place by sticking the pinwheel onto the rubber end of a pencil with a drawing pin.

* * *

Once finished, simply blow!

REVERSE PICKPOCKET

Reverse pickpocketing, the art of putting things in people's pockets without them noticing, is a very amusing way to fill an afternoon when it's looking a bit grubby outside. The aim of the game is to silently and stealthily get as many 'things' into your family and friends' pockets as you can. If you discover something in your pocket, you're not allowed to take it out until the end of day. We played this endlessly on a recent skiing holiday with friends and it provided the entertainment and amusement for the week. The only downside was that everyone had the frustrating task of emptying their pockets and replacing the items back around the house at the end of each day. Count up items over dinner to find the winner. If you want to get really competitive about it, put differently coloured stickers on the items before planting them in people's pockets to mark out who's reverse pickpocketed what.

DUST OFF THE BOARD GAMES

If your board games have been gathering dust at the back of the cupboard for the past few years then dig them out and remind yourself of the bonding fun that they instantly provide. If you're bored of the ones you have, then head to your local charity shop where there is always a range of novelty ones available for tuppence. I spent one rain-soaked camping holiday in Wales holed up in a tent for a week playing endless rounds of 'Find the Treasure', a brilliant little game I picked up from the local village jumble sale.

HOUSE GYMNASTICS

If you're itching for something a little more energetic then why not give house gymnastics a go. Developed by some enterprising young men called Harrison and Ford, who were inspired when working out how best to hang a blind, this energetic activity involves manoeuvring yourself around the home using a combination of various disciplines including yoga, breakdancing and climbing. These intrepid characters have even set up a website to inspire you to get stuck into the sport. Visit www. housegymnastics.com. Or better yet, invent your own ways of getting around the house or doing the housework – try the splits while doing the dusting!

ELLIE'S BRILLIANT NAME GAME

This is one of my favourite after dinner games – it has travelled around the world with me and has proved a hit wherever and whenever it's rolled out. The game involves having to communicate as many names as possible by either describing, using one word or miming to give clues to them. Here's how to play:

> Each player tears a piece of paper into between five and ten small pieces (depending on how long you want the game to go on for) and writes the name of a famous person – fictional or real – on each. All the slips of paper are folded and then put into a hat or bowl in the middle of the table.

* * *

The team going first chooses a player to start, who takes a piece of paper from the hat and describes the person to the rest of their team without mentioning any part of their name. They can do anything but say the name on the paper: impressions and 'sounds like' clues are allowed.

* * *

They continue doing this for one minute, describing as many names as they can get through. If their team guesses correctly, that name goes into a small pile. If they can't get it, it goes back in the hat. At the end of the sixty seconds, the number of correct guesses is counted up and this is the player's score. Names that have been correctly guessed are put aside.

* * *

It's then someone on the next team's turn and the game continues, rotating through teams and team members until all the names in the hat have been used up.

* * *

The game then moves into round two. It's almost exactly the same as the first round, but this time team members are only allowed to say a one-word clue. For example, if the famous person was Marilyn Monroe and it was mentioned in the previous round that 'she was the film star who stood on the grille with her skirt blowing up', then you might choose to simply say 'skirt' in the second round.

* * *

In the final round players have to mime each famous name, hoping that their teammates remember them from the two previous rounds.

* * *

The team with the highest overall score wins.

———— THE BOOK GAME ————

This is a brilliant game to play if you've hired a holiday cottage, as there is often an eclectic and sometimes comedic collection of books that past guests have left behind. You can, of course, play it wherever you like – you just need an obscure or unpredictable selection of books to make it as interesting as possible. Here's what to do:

Gather your selection of books and put them in the middle of the table. Ensure each player has a pad and pen.

* * *

Players take it in turns to lead a round, each selecting a book and reading out the title, author's name and blurb if there is one. The rest of the players must then imagine what the book's first line might be and write it down. The object of the game is to dupe the rest of the players into thinking your first line is the real one.

* * *

Whoever is leading the round must also write down the actual first line before collecting everyone else's. They must then take each one and read them out in turn, as convincingly as possible.

∗

Players must guess which one they think is the real first line. Points are awarded as follows:

Two points if someone guesses the right line

One point to a player if someone chooses their fake opening line

If nobody picks the true first line then the person who is leading that round scores two points

Finally, players get five points if they somehow manage to write down the correct first line of the book. It sounds unlikely but it has happened!

∗

The game rotates with each person taking their turn to lead.

∗

One thing to remember is that it's important for everyone to write as clearly as possible, since if the leader of the round can't decipher the writing when they read the words out, it will be obvious that they're fake.

DINNER TABLE
COIN CURLING

If it's still raining outside why not clear the dinner table and convert it to a coin curling court. You'll need a long table (the longer the better), some chalk and two coins per player. Next, draw three circles at one end of the table, one inside the other, slowly decreasing in size. Issue all the players with their coins, ensuring they are the same denomination to prevent calls of foul play. The aim of the game is to get your coins as near to the centre of the circle as possible by propelling them down from the other end of the table with a flicking motion. Once all the coins have been played, the person with a coin closest to the very centre of the smallest circle is the winner. One point is awarded for a win, and there's an additional point available if both your coins are beating everyone else. First to 20 is the overall winner.

The way to ensure summer in England is to have it framed and glazed in a comfortable room.
Horace Walpole

Culture And Leisure In The Great Outdoors

> *All the world's a stage,*
> *And all the men and women merely players.*
> William Shakespeare, *As You Like It*

In recent years summer social calendars have been filled with more outdoor festivals and cultural events than have ever been seen before. Each new season sees the arrival of a list of fledgling music festivals, or new initiatives by leading cultural providers wanting to add an al fresco touch to their performance schedules. We have seen cinemas taken to city parks and squares, theatrical performances in places we didn't even know existed and art exhibitions that re-invent spaces that have previously been written off. This burst of new energy has invigorated Britain's love of culture in all its forms. It has found new audiences and has opened the way for a fresh perspective to be given to dusty, archaic formats.

To help ensure you have a culturally splendid summer to remember, this chapter features details of some of our country's most celebrated events. I have restricted my choices to those occasions that allow you to be out and about in our fantastic countryside, and events that take place each year to ensure there is something to keep you coming back. The chapter has been divided into four sections: theatre, film, festivals and alternative days out. May your summer weekends be immersed in culture and sunshine.

THEATRE

When the sun is riding high in the sky, the last place you want to head for an evening's entertainment is the stale interior of a fusty theatre. So liberate your theatre-going experience and sample some of our country's outdoor dramatic delights:

STAMFORD SHAKESPEARE SEASON
The Stamford Shakespeare Company presents an annual season of plays in June, July and August at Rutland Open Air Theatre in the grounds of historic Tolethorpe Hall, Stamford. The theatre dates back some 800 years and is set in an enchanting glade in the grounds of the estate. Fine actors, stunning sets, gorgeous costumes and majestic surroundings make for a magical warm summer evening spent enjoying dramatic productions in the great outdoors. For those keen to make the most of their

experience, you can arrive early to enjoy a picnic in the grounds before the show. The program usually includes performances of classics such as *Romeo and Juliet* and *Richard III*, and there is always a contemporary twist to keep people coming back for more.

THE EDINBURGH FRINGE FESTIVAL

This falls both into midsummer and late summer, as it stretches through the month of August. Set up as a side event to the original Edinburgh International Festival, the Fringe has now grown to be bigger and better known than it's older sibling. Its size has burgeoned to such an extent that it is now the biggest arts festival in the world. Every year, over three weeks in August, thousands of performers take to a multitude of stages large and small all over Edinburgh to present shows covering the full cultural spectrum. From big names in the world of entertainment to unknown artists looking to build their careers, the festival features theatre, comedy, dance, physical theatre, musicals, operas, concerts, exhibitions and a whole host of things you didn't even know existed.

CORNWALL'S MINACK THEATRE

The Minack Theatre was planned, built and financed in the thirties and forties by one enterprising and determined theatre lover, Rowena Cade. This architecturally stunning theatre has been carved into the rock face overlooking Porthcurno Bay in Cornwall. Audiences can enjoy leading companies and actors performing against the backdrop of crashing waves. *The Tempest* was the first play to be performed in this dramatic space in 1932. Shakespeare continues to be a central focus to every season at the Minack, alongside an impressive and diverse programme of theatrical and musical offerings.

REGENT'S PARK OPEN AIR THEATRE, LONDON

The Open Air Theatre in London's Regent's Park has been a permanent feature since 1932. With one of the largest auditoria in London, it is the oldest professional, permanent outdoor theatre in Britain. Its annual 16-week season is attended by over 130,000 people each year and provides Londoners and visitors with the chance to enjoy some of our country's leading actors and performances in the magical al fresco surroundings of one London's most popular parks. The programme is wide and varied and includes everything from *Lord of the Flies* to stand-up comedy from top-name comics. For more information visit www.openairtheatre.org.

THE DUKES, LANCASTER

Since 1986, The Dukes theatre in Lancaster has prided itself on presenting the 'biggest open-air walkabout theatre event in the UK'. This annual extravaganza takes place at Williamson Park in the centre of the city every summer, and features a diverse programme which includes national productions as well as more local work.

NATIONAL TRUST PROPERTIES

Each year the National Trust puts on an impressive programme of outdoor theatre events at stately homes, castles and other historic properties up and down the country. The programme offers a wide variety that has included *Beauty and the Beast* at Culzean Castle, one of Scotland's grandest homes, and *Romeo and Juliet* at Corfe Castle, Dorset's most majestic medieval ruin.

SHAKESPEARE'S GLOBE, LONDON

London's South Bank hosts an atmospheric recreation of Shakespeare's Elizabethan theatre that enables visitors to experience productions in the same environment as back in Shakespeare's day, minus the stench of body odour and bad breath. Well, that does depend on who you are sitting next to! You can either get sheltered seats in case it rains or, if you want the full 16th-century experience, you can buy a cheap ticket and stand with the other 'groundlings' in the pit.

NATIONAL BOTANIC GARDEN OF WALES, CARMARTHENSHIRE

Each year, The National Botanic Garden of Wales puts on a selection of open-air performances to be enjoyed as part of their summer events calendar. Favourites have included *A Midsummer Night's Dream* and *Alice Through the Looking Glass*. Visitors are encouraged to bring rugs, picnics and wine for a magical evening in these dazzling gardens. For more information visit www.gardenofwales.org.uk.

THE DELL, STRATFORD-UPON-AVON

To get as close to the man himself as possible, head to Shakespeare's home town for free outdoor theatre throughout the summer. The Royal Shakespeare Company's outdoor space, The Dell, hosts a programme of lively student and amateur productions.

FILM

Why waste a summer's evening inside watching a film when the same experience can be enjoyed so much more outdoors. Below is a guide to some of our countries best al fresco cinematic experiences.

SCREENFIELDS, MANCHESTER
Screenfields is Manchester city centre's free open-air cinema, and it attracts over 60,000 film-goers each year. The programme usually shows a mix of classics, comedies, dramas and 'dress-up' films every Thursday evening from May to September. Even better than that, all performances are free.

THE SCOOP, LONDON
The Scoop is London's permanent riverside amphitheatre built in front of City Hall. As well as an impressive programme of cultural performances, The Scoop also shows frcc films throughout the summer. More information can be found on The Scoop's website at www.morelondon.com.

SOMERSET HOUSE, LONDON
Another London offering, this one set against the impressive backdrop of Somerset House. The programme usually features

classics alongside more contemporary offerings and attracts everyone from celebrities to tourists passing through the capital.

SYON PARK, LONDON

Enjoy an al fresco film in the beautiful and calm surroundings of Syon Park, located a stone's throw away from the crowds and fumes of central London. There is a bar and the film programme is usually an eclectic mix of old classics and summertime hits. For more information visit www.syonpark.co.uk.

—— FESTIVAL FUN ——

Festivals have become a prerequisite feature of any discerning cultural consumer's social calendar. These days its hard to stroll anywhere during a British summer without tripping over one. To help you separate the wheat from the chaff, I've picked some of the best for you to enjoy:

CAMBRIDGE FOLK FESTIVAL

The Cambridge Folk Festival is an annual celebration of all that is folk that takes place in Cherry Hinton Hall in Cambridgeshire. It's renowned for its eclectic mix of artists and it takes place over a long summer weekend.

PORT ELIOT FESTIVAL

This festival takes place in the majestic setting of the Port Eliot estate near Plymouth and offers a rich platter of arts including music, literature, poetry, food, comedy, film and art alongside a host of other eccentricities. You can relax inside the stunning walled gardens, eat home-made cake in a beautiful Orangery, get sucked into spontaneous performances in some of the most suprising places, dance into the wee small hours, laugh until it hurts, or perhaps explore the estate in the moonlight with a moon-watching guide.

LATITUDE

Latitude is an annual culture and music festival that turns the outdoors into a stage. Designed for the festival-goer who is seeking a little more than a hedonistic escape, Latitude includes live music from leading artists, poetry readings, artistic installations, comedy, cabaret, politics, dance and literature.

GLASTONBURY

Glastonbury is the worldwide king of music festivals. Set in the idyllic Somerset countryside on Michael Eavis's Worthy Farm in Pilton, Glastonbury has been going and growing since the 1970s. The festival normally takes place on the last full weekend of June. It features a diverse and impressive programme of music and has been the launch pad for many new and now major artists. Tickets are like gold dust and sell out many months in advance. If you manage to get your hands on one, be prepared for an assault on and potential loss of your senses. To get the most out of it, dive straight in.

BESTIVAL

Bestival is a bit like a giant house party in a field that transports otherwise sensible 20 and 30 somethings back to their wild teenage years. The event takes place over three days in Robin Hill Country Park on the Isle of Wight. It has been running since 1994 and continues to win plaudits. If you can get hold of a ticket expect to take part in giant fancy dress parades, party games and various eccentric workshops and activities.

——— ALTERNATIVE ———
SUMMER DAYS OUT

If you're looking for something a little different from the norm, then here are some ideas for brilliant alternative summer days out:

LARPING

LARPING, otherwise known as live action role-playing, is essentially a live game where players are in full costume and have to act out their character's roles, make decisions and experience the consequences. It's a little bit odd to see lots of grown men and women 'playing' with such vigour, but once you embrace the whole ethos it has the potential to transport you to another world like nothing else. Many of the participants take it very seriously and it enables them to spend some of their life in a parallel universe. If you or your kids love a spot of Tolkein or today's equivalent, then LARPING should be just your cup of tea. Do a bit of research and speak to the different LARP providers, and make sure you find a group where first-timers or children are welcome. You'll find useful information at www.live-roleplaying. co.uk and www.heroquest-larp.co.uk.

FOSSIL AND DINOSAUR WALKS, ISLE OF WIGHT
The Isle of Wight was once home to more than a dozen species of dinosaur – the biggest concentration known in Europe. You can do some dinosaur hunting yourself with the Dinosaur Isle team who organise two-hour fossil walks all summer. The walks are led by museum specialists at three different sites: Yaverland, Shanklin and Brook Bay. Loose fossils can be picked up and dinosaur evidence will be pointed out.

HERITAGE OPEN DAYS
Heritage Open Days offer a single long-weekend celebration of England's impressive architecture and culture. Over four days in September they offer free access to properties that are usually closed to the public or normally charge for admission. From castles to factories, town halls to tithe barns, parish churches to Buddhist temples, you will be able to discover hidden architectural treasures and learn more about England's history. For exact dates and venues visit www.heritageopendays.org.uk.

GO GHOST HUNTING

For those intrigued by things that go bump in the night, ghost hunting is a fantastic alternative way to spend an evening. Up and down the UK, there are houses and cemeteries wrapped with ghoulish history where sightings and other paranormal activities are common. If you're in London then head to the eerie, crooked gravestones and headless angels of Highgate Cemetery. Essex is home to the famous 18th-century ghost hunter Harry Price, who got involved in a case at Borley Rectory that led it to be named 'The Most Haunted House in England'. If you fancy spending an evening being scared out of your wits, do a spot of Internet research to find the most haunted place in your area and pay it a visit.

THE EDEN PROJECT

The Eden Project is now one of Cornwall's greatest tourist attractions. Built in a reclaimed kaolin pit 3 miles outside St Austell, the complex offers the world's largest covered conservatories (or biomes), and nothing prepares you for the sheer scale of it. Visitors can wander through a tropical rainforest complete with waterfalls or take a stroll through the Mediterranean zone where perfumed citrus trees, vines, banks of crops and a riot of colourful blooms recreate another world. For tickets and more information visit www.edenproject.com.

BLACKPOOL ILLUMINATIONS

At 10 kilometres long and using over one million bulbs, the Blackpool Illuminations are an awesome spectacle and well worth a visit. Consisting of every kind of light display you can imagine – lasers, neon, light bulbs, fibre optics, searchlights and floodlighting –

it's an astounding sight (and the organisers have been making efforts to make the event more environmentally friendly). The 'Big Switch On', usually a celebrity-hosted event, takes place in early September and the lights are on display each evening all the way through to early November. For more information go to www.visitblackpool.com.

LAKE WINDERMERE BY STEAMBOAT

A visit to Cumbria would be missing a trick were it without a visit to England's largest inland body of water, Lake Windermere. At over 10 miles long and 1 mile wide, the lake has the appearance of a large river. The best way to explore its verdant coves and deep inky waters is by boat. Steamboats have run on the lake for over 150 years and allow you to explore the town of Windermere, the historic fortress of Wray Castle and the former home of Beatrix Potter. Windermere Lake Cruises (www.windermere-lakecruises. co.uk) offer a great choice of cruises; alternatively, contact Windermere Tourist Information for other providers (www. lakelandgateway.info).

XSCAPE, GLASGOW

Those Scots are a hardy outdoor bunch. Not to be stalled by their notoriously inclement weather, they have created an extravaganza of indoor entertainment in the form of Xscape, which offers all of the outdoor sports you could ever want in the comfort of an indoor complex. There's the soccer circus offering a fully automated football shooting range, and even a minigolf course on a paradise island. Winter sports enthusiasts won't be disappointed either as they can enjoy real snow all year round and have a go at snowboarding, skiing, ice skating and even a daring ice slide. It's also home to Britain's largest free-standing climbing wall as well as the Skypark, an aerial adventure course set 15 metres above the ground. After all that entertainment, you can finish your day in the state-of-the-art cinema or meander around the impressive selection of shops, cafes and restaurants.

Share The Summer Love

Summer is a time to bathe yourself in fresh air and spend some quality time with those you love. It's also a perfect opportunity to meet new people and get involved with your local community. Sadly, for the past few decades, cities have become infamous for their lack of neighbourly relations. City folk spend decades living side-by-side on the same street with barely a nod of greeting, let alone an offer of support. Thankfully, the idea of 'community' is beginning to reassert itself: creative types have been organising free community festivals, the National Trust puts on giant picnics and there has been a resurgence of Coronation-style street parties. In the same way that we have been looking back to past generations to learn how to live more frugally, growing our own food and darning our socks, this deep-seated nostalgia is now also extending to the way we interact and engage with those around us.

If you fancy putting a bit of community back into your summer then this chapter will hopefully inspire and lead you on your way. From organising community events to the smaller stuff that you can do, you should find a few ideas to at least encourage some supportive exchanges with your neighbours and help you to bring a spot of good old-fashioned community back into your life.

SET UP
A
FACEBOOK PAGE

Love it or hate it, Facebook is a fantastic vehicle to share information with large groups, and people are learning to use it as a means to promote more than their own social life. It has proved itself an impressive way to gain support for charitable causes, for example. In the same way, Facebook is also a fantastic portal for promoting and discussing community matters. By setting up a Facebook page for your town, village, street or community, you can easily share news, raise concerns or even trade (in anything from babysitting to sofas). It's also the ideal medium to advertise community parties and events.

Local Facebook sites give people a reason to interact and a subject to engage over and can act as a stepping-stone to some quality face-to-face meetings. If you fancy setting a page up then follow the simple instructions on Facebook and it'll be done in five minutes. Once you've set it up, produce some flyers and post them through your neighbours' doors telling them to sign up and become a 'friend' of the community. In a couple of clicks, they'll have access to your burgeoning social network.

STAND UP
FOR YOUR ———
COMMUNITY RIGHTS

With government cutbacks continuing with vigour, local initiatives, buildings and activities have been some of the first victims to suffer. In line with the new era of community spirit described above, I believe that one of the key responses we will see is a movement of politically and socially active campaigners and community-minded folk taking control.

If you want to stand up for your community then why not start your own campaign: whether it's about building allotments on old boat hulls in city canals or campaigning to keep Meals on Wheels in your area, it's a fantastic way to have a positive impact and help others along the way. Below are a few tips to get you started:

* * *

Define your objectives and focus. Find a way to succinctly describe what you're trying to achieve in a short sentence that is both compelling and persuasive.

* * *

Arm yourself with information. Research your subject and know it inside out. Try to find other supporters with specialist knowledge who can join your campaign.

It's very useful, for example, to have a lawyer as part of your group who might be able to help identify legal loopholes, or a surveyor who can vouch for the safety of a condemned piece of local architectural heritage.

* * *

Find out who are the people who can make a difference. It might be the local councillors who will be making the casting vote, or your MP who has the power to stop or make something happen. Once you've identified them, get in touch and explain what you're trying to achieve and why.

* * *

If your local issue is to do with lack of funds, then research what grants might be available and start the process of application. There are a huge number of trusts and foundations set up to address a whole host of social issues ranging from preserving heritage and wildlife to improving social welfare. There are funding search websites that can help you identify what's out there.

* * *

Recruit for support. This might involve setting up a Facebook page for your campaign or encouraging parents at your local school to sign up, for example. You'll need to regularly report on progress to drive awareness and support. You can also try to secure press coverage in the local paper or on community websites, or you could hand out leaflets to people as they walk past in the area you're campaigning for.

* * *

As more people express an interest in supporting your issue, set up a committee of individuals who regularly meet and share out tasks.

* * *

Those who don't have the time to be on the committee can become ambassadors: provide them with the materials and information they'll need to raise awareness amongst their contacts and help fight your cause.

* * *

Finally, understand your opposition. The key to success will be to win over those who are against you.

PUT ON
A
STREET PARTY

The re-emergence of street parties is one of the driving forces behind the return of 'community', and with a royal wedding in 2011, it was like the Queen's coronation all over again. If you fancy getting to know your neighbours and injecting a spot of community into where you live then organising a street party is a great place to start. To help you on your way visit www.streetsalive. org.uk, where you can find a whole host of tips and advice. You never know who you might meet.

HOLD A VILLAGE
— OR —
STREET FETE

Village fêtes are another community spirited event to have benefitted from the burst of interest in all things neighbourly. These once rather obligatory and uninspiring affairs are now being re-invigorated with new enthusiasm and support. If your village, town or street is without one, then why not lead the charge? Here are a few tips to help you get started:

* * *

Start planning your event a long time in advance: January or even earlier would be ideal for a midsummer event. Advanced planning and research is the difference between something that feels cobbled together and an event that immediately makes its mark as an annual feature of your village, town or street social calendar.

* * *

Set up a committee of individuals representing a cross-section of your community and brainstorm the format of the event and what each person can do to make it a success. Approach your local school(s), church(es) and shop(s) and ask them if they will get involved. Get them to sponsor an activity or run a stall (but make sure it's something that will attract people to come along).

* * *

Make sure you have all the necessary safety, legal and insurance procedures in place. The best place to start is to contact your local council and let them know the full details of your event. They will be able to give you all the information you'll need.

* * *

Decide what attractions you're going to have. It might be that you're going to pack the day with competitions such as the largest vegetable, the dog that looks most like their owner or the best jam. There's nothing like a spot of competition to inspire people to come along and get involved. You also need to make sure you have a host of games and activities to entertain those who will just be there to enjoy the day. Traditional village fête games include welly wanging, a tombola, a coconut shy, and so on. You can also shake things up with alternative entertainments such as toe wrestling or a human fruit machine.

* * *

Finally, make sure you promote your event far and wide to ensure the biggest attendance possible.

Contact your local newspaper, get in touch with community websites, put notices and posters up in public places, local shops and on lamp posts, and provide everyone with images and copy so that they can advertise the day on social network sites. Submit the details to as many websites as possible that upload information for free: *Country Life* magazine publishes a Village Fête Calendar and the Innocent smoothie people also help promote local village fêtes (see www. innocentvillagefete.com).

BOUNTY BARTER

This is a fantastic idea the National Trust promote. It will appeal to anyone with a glut of chutneys, jams, apples and courgettes from an over-exuberant burst of culinary activity or from a particularly fruitful year. The idea is to hold an event where everyone brings along their extra produce and swaps and shares to their heart's content. You might want to just organise it with friends over a lunch party or you could take it a step further and run a bounty barter as a stall at your village fête or street party.

ORGANISE
—— A FARMERS' MARKET ——
IN YOUR AREA

Farmers' markets are proving to be a central hub of community activity and for many towns and villages a key tourist attraction as well. The idea of buying your produce direct from the farmer, instead of lining the pockets of the middlemen has a huge appeal. You also know the provenance of your goods and can question the producers to understand exactly what's been put in the foods to achieve the perfection you see before you. If you don't have a farmers' market in your area, then follow these simple steps to see if you can get one started:

* * *

Do your research. Be clear about why you want to set up a farmers' market, what you want to offer and who you're hoping to sell to. Treat it like a marketing plan: research demand in your area by conducting surveys to find out what other locals would like to buy.

* * *

Set up a committee of individuals who can help you. This is a big job and one that is too mammoth for one person alone.

* * *

Identify potential places where the market could be held. Local school fields that aren't used on a Saturday are a great idea. Alternatively, contact your local council to see how they can help. You'll need to speak to them anyway to ensure you address all necessary legal, safety and insurance requirements.

* * *

Find local providers who would be interested in selling at your event. Research farms and producers located in your region and put ads in local agricultural shops, village shops and magazines. The easiest way is to see how other people have done it. If there's another farmers' market that takes place in the next town along, save yourself the work and speak to the organisers to see if you can mirror what they've already achieved.

* * *

Finally, remember that this is a huge task but one that can deliver enormous rewards. The advice given here is only enough to start off – to fully understand the work necessary, it's essential to speak to your local council. You might be surprised as they could be very keen to help.

COMMUNITY COMPETITION

In testament to the classic Jones's rivalry, why not organise a community competition that encourages households of all ages to get involved. These age-old events have been organised by many villages in the UK and across Europe for years. There's the Pucklechurch Scarecrow competition, for example, or my local rubber duck race. Both are big successes and mark a key date in the community calendar. You could organise a front-door-decorating competition to mark the midsummer solstice or a barbecue-off to see who's got the best burger-flipping skills on the street. Or why not take a leaf out of the WI book and hold a cake-baking competition? Another idea is to pick up on a theme from the area that you live in: if you're by the sea, organise a shrimping or fishing competition, or if you're a city-bound landlubber then how about challenging your neighbours to a dustbin decorating competition to add a touch of sparkle to the traditional grey-green plastic tubs.

HOLD A DOG PARTY

As any city- or town-based dog walker knows, the whole community thing has been busily going on within this group for years. If you're a regular dawn or dusk dog walker then I'm sure you're at least on nodding terms with your fellow dog lovers – you may even know their names, ages and shoe sizes. In the park over the road there is a veritable coffee morning as the regulars gather at the same spot to share pleasantries each day.

Why not 'formalise' this doggy network. One group I know hold an annual summer party where they each bring a canapé-style breakfast to share while their dogs run amok around them. If you fancy getting friendly with your fellow dog walkers, then suggest it to a couple of the ones you see each day. Promote a meeting by putting notices up on trees. You never know where it might lead.

Foraging And Other Fruity Fun

> *As Summer into Autumn slips*
> *And yet we sooner say*
> *'The Summer' than 'the Autumn,' lest*
> *We turn the sun away.*
> Emily Dickinson, 'As Summer Into Autumn Slips'

The season's fruits and foraging mark out the passing of the summer months. The arrival of the creamy flower display on the elderflower bush kicks off the bounty, and the start of elderflower cordial and champagne production (see pages 129–130). Next comes the restocking of redcurrant jelly supplies and a month's worth of gooseberry fool. Late summer ripens the remaining fruit and evenings are spent beating the birds to the best finds. Summer is signed off by the arrival of sloes in the hedgerows and the harvesting and preparation of the sloe gin in anticipation of Christmas celebrations.

I come from a family with an impressive foraging pedigree. Much of my childhood summer was spent scouring hedgerows for blackberries or hunting down reachable wild cherries. I'd race to find the juiciest berries, competing for the prize of the greatest hoard, and would end the day with scratched arms and deep red juice stains. When I was growing up all of this was deeply uncool, but thanks to the ubiquitous Hugh Fearnley-Whittingstall, foraging has enjoyed something of a renaissance over the past decade. Scouring hedgerows is no longer seen as the eccentric behaviour of a mad aunt or barmy uncle. Foraging has become yet another accepted activity that recalls times gone by, a reaction to spend and consume culture.

There is something very satisfying about gathering fruit and foraging for free finds. It's an activity that harks back to a simpler time, and one that appeals to our primal hunter-gatherer instincts. If you fancy having a go at harvesting the bounty of our summer hedgerows and trees, then this chapter gives some advice to get you started and some ideas for recipes.

THE DOS AND ——— DON'TS OF FORAGING ——— AND SCRUMPING

* 1 *

Be careful where you pick from. Avoid polluted main roads or areas that have been sprayed with insecticides. Stick to public woods, hedgerows, footpaths, towpaths and city parks.

* 2 *

Don't steal from private land. You must stick to public highways and byways.

* 3 *

Know what you're eating. Don't rely purely on illustrations: read whatever guidebook you have too, and if you want to be super scrupulous, look at several different texts. I always use Richard Mabey's *Food for Free*. You can also get your hands on a host of brilliant mobile phone applications to help you identify foraging finds.

* 4 *

Only pick a small amount from each tree and make sure you leave plenty for the birds and wildlife. Never pick the flowers or seeds of annual plants as they rely on them for survival.

* 5 *

Take along a pair of thorn-proof gloves so your hands aren't lacerated when you reach into difficult spots for the best fruit.

THE
BEST BLACKBERRY
JAM

After years of failed attempts to gather enough blackberries from our local park, I was delighted to discover my very own blackberry bush when I was given my allotment a couple of years ago. The mild temperatures and damp climate of 2010's summer proved to be a bumper year for fruit and I managed to make gallons of beautiful blackberry jam. Here's my well-practiced recipe:

Ingredients
A large quantity of foraged blackberries
Sugar
1 apple, grated
Juice of 2 lemons

1. To get started, sterilise some jam jars by following the instructions on page 126. Put a couple of small saucers in the fridge or freezer too (you'll need these to test your jam to see if it has set).

2. Pick through your fruit and throw away any blackberries that are past their best. Weigh the fruit

you have left and put it in a large pan with half that amount of sugar and the apple (which, with its high pectin levels, will help the setting process).

3. Gently heat the blackberries through on a low heat until all the sugar is dissolved. Then turn up the heat and bring the jam to a rolling boil. This is the point at which the heat in the centre of the pan is just right to make the jam roll continuously out in a circle.

4. Add the lemon juice, to make sure your jam isn't too sweet.

5. After five minutes, test to see if your jam is set using the wrinkle test. Take a saucer from the fridge and drop a small amount of the jam onto it. Leave it to cool for a few minutes and if the surface of the jam wrinkles when pushed with a finger then your jam has reached setting point and is ready to jar. Mine always takes much longer than the recommended five minutes and I've been known to keep the rolling boil going for a good half an hour before setting point has been reached.

6. Leave to cool for 10 minutes and then start ladling the jam into your sterilised jars. Seal and label.

PICKLED PEARS

I fell in love with pickled pears when they were presented as a Christmas treat on the cheese board. The sharp sweet taste of the vinegary pear worked magic on the stilton and it was a taste sensation that certainly earned its place in my annual pickling and jamming calendar. My first failed attempt at pickled pears used some fruit from my friend's garden, but the softness of the pear variety meant they turned to mush. As such, it's important that you use barely ripe conference pears for this recipe.

Ingredients
20 conference pears
Zest of 1 lemon
10 cloves
2 star anise
2 cinnamon sticks
1 tsp all spice berries
5cm ginger
500g brown sugar
1l white wine vinegar

1. Start by sterilising two large 1.5l kilner jars using the sterilisation method. Depending on the size of your pears, you may not fill both, so it's a good idea to have a half-sized sterilised jar ready just in case.

2. Next, put all the ingredients apart from the pears in a pan. Gently warm until all the sugar has dissolved and then bring to the boil.

3. Peel the pears leaving the stalks in place, add them to the pan and gently simmer for about 15 to 20 minutes. Then take them out with a slotted spoon and carefully place them in your sterilised jars top to tail.

4. Meanwhile, increase the heat on the remaining juices in the pan and reduce down by about a third to create a thicker syrupy liquid and then pour this over your jarred pears. Seal and store. They will be ready to eat after a fortnight and will need to be consumed within a couple of months.

———— WILD CHERRY JAM ————

I was staggered to discover how many wild cherry trees there are in the parks and towpaths around where I live. When you think how much you pay for cherries in the shop it's an absolute wonder why more people aren't making the most of this native wild fruit. One small barrier is the fact that the cherry tree generally holds its fruit quite high up, making it a little difficult for non-winged species such as humans to get to it. Once I've located a good tree, I generally bring a stepladder along and spend half an hour helping myself to the dark red fruits, quite often eating as many as I pick. This can draw a few odd looks, but you get used to that after a while. The recipe below is for a superb and hard to purchase cherry treat, wild cherry jam:

Ingredients
2kg cherries
1.2kg sugar
Juice of 2 lemons
1 apple, grated

1. Wash and de-stone the cherries (a boring but necessary job) and then put them into a large pan with the sugar, lemon juice and apple.

2. Heat gently through until all the sugar has dissolved, then bring to a rolling boil.

3. Test to see if your jam will set after five minutes by dropping a small amount onto a chilled saucer. If the

surface of the jam wrinkles when touched then it has reached setting point and is ready to jar. If it hasn't (and, again, mine never has after five minutes) put it back on the boil and keep testing it every five minutes until setting point is reached.

4. Leave to cool for five minutes and then pour into sterilised jam jars. This recipe makes enough jam to fill about 5 to 7 jars.

CRAB APPLE JELLY

This is one of the easiest preserves to make as the high pectin levels of crab apples mean that it sets very easily. Crab apples are another prolific wild fruit that are easily identified as they look like small apples and as no one seems to want to eat them, you'll find trees laden with bountiful fruit all over the place. You will need a jelly bag or muslin cloth to strain out all of the bits and ensure a clear result, but don't let this put you off as the golden end product is a delicious accompaniment to cold meats, roasts and cheeses. This same recipe can be made using quinces instead (the pulp by-product of which can also be turned into quince cheese – see page 199).

Ingredients
4kg crab apples
1kg sugar
Juice of 1 lemon

1. Pick through the apples and remove any leaves or ones that are a little past their best, and then give them a good wash before putting them in a large pan and cover them with water. Slowly bring to the boil and then turn down to simmer gently for about 30 minutes or until the fruit has gone pulpy and soft.

2. Next, spoon the mixture into a jelly bag or into a colander lined with a muslin cloth. Suspend over a large pan and leave to strain through. It's important that you don't try to force the liquid through as this can make it cloudy – let it happen at its own speed.

3. When it's finally drained through (I usually leave it overnight), add the sugar and lemon juice and slowly bring to the boil whilst occasionally stirring. Once the sugar is dissolved, leave it at a rolling boil for anywhere between 20 and 40 minutes or until setting point is reached (see the blackberry jam recipe on page 191 for instructions). As it's boiling, the mixture will regularly create a scum on the top that you need to remove (to prevent it clouding your jelly). Once setting point is reached, pour into sterilised jam jars, seal and store in a cool dark place. Unopened, the jelly should keep for at least a year as long as you have done your sterilising thoroughly.

SPICY FIG COMPOTE

At home on the houseboat, we have a voluptuously laden fig tree that hangs over and crushes the garden fence and that towards the end of the summer makes me writhe with guilt at all the uneaten fruit going to waste. As I've never been a huge fan of figs, it took a lot of research and testing to finally find a good recipe, and this one is a definite hit. These spicy figs are perfect served with cheese and a downright necessity with cooked duck of any kind:

Ingredients
1kg figs
1 small onion, chopped
2 cloves
1 ½ cinnamon sticks
500g caster sugar
300ml white wine vinegar
300ml water
2cm ginger, chopped
Pinch of salt

1. Put all the ingredients apart from the figs into a pan and cook slowly over a low heat until all the sugar has dissolved. Take off the heat.

2. Wash the figs and remove the stalks, then add to the pan and bring back to the boil. Continue boiling for five minutes, then transfer to sterilised jars.

QUINCE CHEESE

Don't worry, I haven't got my fruit and cheese in a twist! This is cheese by name but not by nature. Quince cheese is a classic Spanish accompaniment to their delicious manchego, and is equally delicious with other cheeses of your choice. It's block form, which gives it its name, means that you can slice it up into slabs which can then be wrapped in greaseproof paper and tied with string to make a fantastic dinner party gift. If you're lucky enough to have access to a quince tree then it would be a crime to let them go to waste. Alternatively, you can usually buy quinces from good-quality greengrocers and even some supermarkets.

Ingredients
1kg quinces
Rind of 1 lemon
Juice of ½ lemon
Sugar

1. Roughly chop the quinces, place in a pan and cover with just enough water that they start to float. Add the lemon rind, put on a lid and simmer gently for 2 hours.

2. When the mixture has turned a slightly darker colour, strain through a jelly bag or muslin cloth overnight. You can use the liquid to make quince jelly (see the recipe for crab apple on page 196–7) but for this recipe you need the fruity pulp left over.

3. Weigh the pulp and put it in the pan with the same weight of sugar and the juice of half a lemon. Heat and stir gently until all the sugar is dissolved, then leave it on the lowest hob setting for another 2 hours until the mixture has darkened and become very thick.

4. Grease a baking tray and spoon the liquid into it. Leave to cool and set in a dark place. Once ready, cut into slabs. Quince cheese is best used within two months.

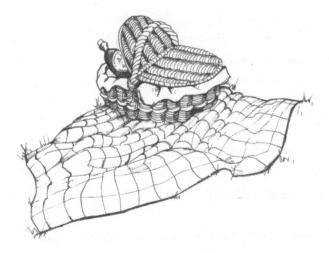

—— REAL ——
RASPBERRY JELLY

Why bother eating packet jelly full of all sorts of nasties when you can make the real organic version in two shakes of a lamb's tail. This real raspberry jelly is absolutely delicious:

Ingredients
250g raspberries
850ml water
250g caster sugar
10g gelatin

1. Put the raspberries, water and caster sugar into a pan and heat gently until the sugar has dissolved. Bring to the boil and continue boiling until the volume has reduced by a third. Take off the heat and leave to cool.

2. Stir in the gelatin and then pour the liquid into a jelly mould – you can strain it if you don't want the bits of fruit to be included. Any large bowl will do if you haven't got a mould.

3. Put the jelly in the fridge for at least half an hour to set. To remove it from the mould, rest it in warm water for a few minutes, put a plate on top, and flip upside down.

4. Serve with a sprinkling of fresh raspberries.

Epilogue

As the long days of summer draw to a close, it's time to pack the deckchairs away and stow the garden bunting for next year. Whether your summer has been drenched in rain or bleached by the sun, I hope *The Book of Summer* has helped you find your way to creating some magical summer memories to store away and keep you going through the cold months ahead. With autumn on the horizon, it's time to look forward to crisp mornings walking on a carpet of crunching leaves, or a chance to huddle up at your favourite pub when the sky hangs heavy.

If you didn't manage to find your way to doing a quarter of the things in this book then you have the whole of autumn and winter to plan next summer's season of fun. If the thought of long evenings and log fires doesn't fill you with joy, then keep the spirit of the summer alive by having this book at hand for a fast route back to some fun in the sun. I hope it gives you as much pleasure as I've had in putting it together.

Index

Notes